THE LOW CHOLESTEROL COOKBOOK

THE LOW CHOLESTEROL COOKBOOK

OVER 50 RECIPES, EACH ONE LOW IN CHOLESTEROL AND SATURATED FATS, BUT HIGH IN TASTE AND APPEAL

CONSULTANT EDITOR
CHRISTINE FRANCE

LORENZ BOOKS

This edition first published in 1998 by Lorenz Books
27 West 20th Street, New York, NY 10011

LORENZ BOOKS are available for bulk purchase for sales promotion and for
premium use. For details, write or call the sales director, Lorenz Books,
27 West 20th Street, New York, NY 10011

© Anness Publishing Limited 1998

Lorenz Books is an imprint of
Anness Publishing Limited

ISBN 1 85967 671 5

Publisher: Joanna Lorenz
Senior Cookery Editor: Linda Fraser
Editor: Margaret Malone
Designer: Sara Kidd
Introduction: Christine McFadden
Nutritional Analysis: Wendy Doyle
Photography: Karl Adamson, Edward Allwright, Steve Baxter, James Duncan,
Amanda Heywood, Don Last, Patrick McLeavey, Michael Michaels,
Thomas Odulate and Peter Reilly
Recipes: Catherine Atkinson, Carla Capalbo, Kit Chan, Roz Denny, Christine
France, Shirley Gill, Christine Ingram, Sue Maggs, Annie Nichols, Maggie
Pannell, Laura Washburn and Stephen Wheeler

Printed and bound in Singapore

Most of the recipes in this book have previously appeared in
The Ultimate Low Cholesterol Low Fat Cookbook

1 3 5 7 9 10 8 6 4 2

CONTENTS

INTRODUCTION

Cooking and eating good food is one of life's greatest pleasures. Unfortunately, the foods we tend to enjoy most are often fatty, and certain types of fat raise the level of cholesterol—a substance strongly implicated in heart disease, strokes and high blood pressure.

Cholesterol is found in the cells of humans and animals, and in the food we eat. Body cholesterol is manufactured in the liver and is used to carry essential fatty acids around the bloodstream to various organs. The human body makes all the cholesterol it needs, and any excess accumulates on the walls of the arteries, restricting the passage of blood and oxygen to the heart. This is why a high level of cholesterol in the blood is generally recognized as one of the risk factors in the development of heart disease.

Dietary cholesterol is found in saturated fats and in food derived from animals—meat, egg yolks and dairy products, for instance. Fats derived from vegetables are cholesterol-free. Interestingly, although some low-fat foods, such as shrimp, contain high levels of cholesterol, it seems that blood cholesterol levels are more affected by the amount of saturated fat in the diet than the amount of cholesterol. So it's now thought that shrimp and other shellfish do not greatly increase cholesterol levels even though they contain cholesterol themselves.

Above: Delicious fruit and vegetables—the perfect start to a healthy diet.

When we eat more saturated fat than we need, the body increases cholesterol production, and the excess ends up in the bloodstream. So even a low-cholesterol diet can raise your blood cholesterol if saturated fats aren't reduced as well.

Most of us eat fats in one form or another every day. In fact, we need to consume a small amount to maintain a healthy and balanced diet, but almost everyone—not just the cholesterol-conscious—can afford to, and should, reduce their fat intake, particularly of saturated fats.

By choosing the right types of fat and making small, simple changes to the way you cook and prepare food, you can reduce your overall fat intake quite dramatically and enjoy a low-fat, low cholesterol diet without really noticing any difference.

As you will see, watching your fat and cholesterol intake doesn't necessarily mean dieting and deprivation. *The Low Cholesterol Cookbook* begins with an informative introduction about basic healthy eating guidelines. There are tips on how to cook with fat-free and low-fat ingredients; suggestions about which foods to cut down on and what to try instead; information on the best cook-ware for fat-free cooking; and a compre-hensive fat and calorie content chart.

Here are more than 50 easy-to-follow recipes that your whole family can enjoy. Every recipe has been developed in line with modern nutritional guidelines, and each one has at-a-glance nutritional information so you can instantly check the calorie, saturated fat and cholesterol content. The selection of foods included will surprise you: there are pizza and pastas, tasty sautés and stews, vegetable main courses, fish and seafood dishes galore and delicious breads, cookies and cakes all with less fat than traditional recipes, of course, but packed with flavor and vitality.

Below: Be aware not only of what you eat, but also how much you eat of each of the five food groups.

THE IMPORTANCE OF DIET

A healthy diet is one that provides the body with all the nutrients it needs for growth and repair and to resist disease. To get the balance right, it is important to know just how much to eat of each type of food.

Of the five main food groups (see below), it is recommended that we eat at least five portions of fruit and vegetables a day (excluding potatoes). We should also try to eat a high proportion of energy-producing foods such as cereals, pasta, rice, beans, bread and potatoes; moderate amounts of meat, fish, poultry, eggs and dairy products; and only small amounts of fat and sugar.

THE FIVE MAIN FOOD GROUPS

● Fruit and vegetables
● Cereals, rice, potatoes, beans, bread and pasta
● Meat, poultry, fish and eggs
● Milk and other dairy foods
● Fats, oils and sugars

You can reduce your intake of dietary cholesterol by cutting down on fat, particularly the saturated kind. Aim to limit your daily fat intake to no more than 30 percent of total calories. In real terms, this means that for an average daily intake of 2,000 calories, 30 percent of energy would come from 600 calories. Since each gram of fat provides 9 calories, your total daily intake should be no more than 66.6g fat. Your total intake of saturated fats should be no more than 10 percent of the total calories (that is 6.6g).

TYPES OF FAT

All fats and oils are made up of three units of fatty acids and a unit of glycerol (glycerin). Their individual properties vary according to the type and combination of fatty acids.

All fatty acids are made up of chains of carbon atoms, some or all of which have either one or two hydrogen atoms

Above: Though not all fats are 'bad', only small amounts are needed in the diet.

attached to them. If any of the hydrogen atoms are missing, two carbon atoms join together to form what is known as a double bond. Fatty acids containing one double bond are said to be unsaturated, fatty acids containing more than one double bond are called polyunsaturated, while those with a single double bond are known as monounsaturated. Those containing all the hydrogen atoms they can hold are called saturated fatty acids.

All fats contain both saturated and unsaturated (either poly- or monounsaturated) fatty acids, but if the proportion of saturated is greater than unsaturated, the fat is generally said to be 'saturated', and vice versa.

● *Saturated fats –*
Saturated fats are generally solid at room temperature and are mostly found in foods derived from animal sources. However, there are also saturated fats of vegetable origin, notably coconut and palm oils (although these do not contain cholesterol), as well as some margarines and oils in which some of the unsaturated fatty acids have been processed into saturated ones. These products are labeled 'hydrogenated' and are best avoided.

● *Polyunsaturated fats –*
Polyunsaturated fats are usually liquid at room temperature. There are two types: those of vegetable or plant origin (containing fatty acids known as omega-6), such as nut, seed and vegetable oils and soft margarine; and those from oily fish (omega-3), such as herring and sardines. Small quantities are essential for good health, and ideally, we should consume equal amounts of omega-6 and omega-3 oils. Most of us are deficient in omega-3.

● *Monounsaturated fats –*
Monounsaturated fats are found in foods such as olive oil and canola oil, some nuts such as almonds and walnuts, oily fish and avocados. These fats are thought to help reduce cholesterol levels, and could explain why there is a low incidence of heart disease in countries where those foods form a major part of the diet.

CHOLESTEROL

Although usually associated with fats, cholesterol isn't actually a fat itself; it is a white, waxy material belonging to a group of substances known as lipoproteins. Cholesterol travels around the bloodstream in tiny droplets of lipoprotein, of which there are three densities: very low density lipoproteins (VLDL), low density (LDL) and high density (HDL). When you eat a lot of saturated fats, your liver produces huge quantities of VLDLs and LDLs. Both types are rich in cholesterol and are the culprits when it comes to blocked arteries. HDLs, however, are thought to help prevent clogged arteries. This is why HDLs are sometimes referred to as 'good' and LDL as 'bad'.

The recommended maximum daily intake of cholesterol is 300mg. This may seem like a lot, but it's very easy to exceed the limit if your diet contains high-cholesterol foods (see box).

CUTTING DOWN ON FAT

About one-quarter of the fat we eat comes from meat and meat products, one-fifth from dairy products and margarine, and the rest from cakes, cookies, pastries and other foods. There are also 'hidden' fats in foods such as many nuts, hummus, avocado.

By being aware of high-fat foods and the type of fat in them, and by making simple changes in your eating habits, you can considerably reduce the total fat content of your diet, and thereby control cholesterol levels.

BOOSTING FIBRE

Studies have shown that certain types of fiber can help reduce blood cholesterol and restrict fat absorption. There are about six different types of fiber, and these can be divided into two groups: soluble and insoluble.

Soluble fiber contains pectin, which acts as a binding agent, helping prevent cholesterol from being absorbed. As a result, the liver's store of cholesterol becomes depleted and it takes up cholesterol from the bloodstream, lowering the blood's cholesterol level. Foods containing soluble fiber include oats, buckwheat, beans, apples, prunes and other dried fruit.

Insoluble fibre is made up of cellulose (found in all plant foods) and lignin (a woody substance found in the central core of fibrous vegetables such as old carrots and parsnips).

Unlike most celluloses, lignin helps lower blood cholesterol by binding to bile acids, whose function is to emulsify fat, thus increasing their excretion from the body.

BOOSTING ANTIOXIDANTS

Some scientists now believe that oxidized fat and cholesterol may be linked to some cancers. Antioxidants

CHOLESTEROL CONTENT OF SELECTED FOODS	
	mg cholesterol per 100g
Egg yolk	1,260
Herring roe	575
Whole egg	450
Calves' liver	370
Caviar (bottled)	285
Mayonnaise	260
Butter	230
Squid	225
Shrimp	195
Heavy cream	140
Pork	110
Chicken, dark meat	105
Salami	79
Lamb, lean	74
Chicken, light meat	70
Cheddar cheese	70
Trout	70
Pork, lean	63
Beef, lean	58
Haddock	36

provide powerful protection by destroying destructive molecules known as free radicals, which cause oxidative damage to the cells. They are also thought to prevent 'bad' LDL cholesterol from oxidizing and causing damge to the artery walls.

The main antioxidants are the carotenes (the plant form of vitamin A) found in orange-fleshed fruit and vegetables; vitamin C, found in citrus fruit, sweet peppers and many other fruits and vegetables; vitamin E, found in vegetable oils, seeds and nuts; the minerals selenium, zinc and magnesium; and certain proteins found in the cabbage family, as well as other fruits and vegetables.

Left: Beware of those foods that are high in cholesterol, such as meat and meat products, cream and cheese. The table above provides the cholesterol content of some common foods.

KEY CHOLESTEROL-LOWERING FOODS

Try to include these foods in your daily diet. They all help lower 'bad' LDL cholesterol, which can clog the arteries or oxidize, causing damage to the artery walls. These foods also boost 'good' HDL cholesterol, which removes LDL cholesterol from the bloodstream.

● Fish—Oily fish such as mackerel, sardines, herring, trout and salmon contain valuable fatty acids known as omega-3. These fatty acids boost HDL cholesterol and are widely believed to help prevent heart disease. Try to eat oily fish two to three times a week. Broil or bake in the oven without any extra oil. Sprinkle with lemon or lime juice and chopped fresh herbs.

● Nuts—Although nuts are high in fat, it's the monounsaturated kind that lowers 'bad' LDL cholesterol and discourages it from oxidizing and damaging the artery walls. Nuts are also a valuable source of vitamin E, which protects against oxidative damage. Almonds and walnuts are said to be particularly effective. Eat just a few nuts each day as a snack, or add them to salads or cakes.

● Oats—Just two ounces of oats or oat bran a day, as part of a low-fat diet, is known to dramatically reduce cholesterol. As well as eating oats in oatmeal and muesli, add them to homemade bread and cookies, or sprinkle into crumble toppings. Sprinkle oat bran over yogurt or fruit and sweeten with a little honey.

● Olive oil and canola oil—These oils, particularly olive oil, are very high in monounsaturates, which lower 'bad' LDL cholesterol and prevent it from causing oxidative damage to the arteries. They slightly raise or keep 'good' HDL cholesterol the same. Polyunsaturated oils such as sunflower and corn oil lower both types of cholesterol, so you miss out on the protective power of HDL cholesterol. Use 'pure' olive oil in moderation for cooking and 'extra virgin' for salads.

● Legumes—Countless studies indicate that legumes—dried beans, lentils and chickpeas—work miracles in fighting high cholesterol when eaten on a daily basis. You can use all types of beans: kidney, pinto, small cannellini, lima beans, navy, soy; even ordinary baked beans. Use canned or precooked beans to replace some or all of the meat in stews; add cooked beans to hearty salads and soups; or whirl them in a blender with garlic, lemon, herbs and a little olive oil to make dips and pâtés.

Below: Certain foods boost 'good' cholesterol while reducing the 'bad'.

FRESH FRUIT AND VEGETABLES

Including plenty of fruit and vegetables in your diet—ideally at least five portions daily (excluding potatoes)—will help control cholesterol levels. Almost all are naturally fat-free as well as providing carotene (the plant form of vitamin A), vitamins C and E, minerals and dietary fiber.

Apples: A useful source of energy-giving carbohydrate, vitamin C and pectin (a soluble fiber thought to lower cholesterol).

Apricots: An excellent source of carotene and cholesterol-lowering soluble fiber.

Bananas: Packed with carbohydrates, bananas are a fat-free energy booster. Slice and add to yogurt, breakfast cereal and muesli, or spread on wholewheat toast.

Citrus fruit: An excellent source of vitamin C and carotene (antioxidants that may help minimize the risk of heart disease). Pectin in the flesh and fibrous membranes is thought to help lower blood cholesterol.

Grapes: Red and black grapes are rich in bioflavonoids (antioxidants that may help protect against heart disease and some cancers).

Kiwi fruit: Kiwis are an excellent source of vitamin C and also provide pectin, a cholesterol-lowering soluble fibre.

Mangoes: Wonderful mixed with yogurt or in a tropical fruit salad, mangoes are packed with beta carotene, vitamin C and soluble fiber.

Prunes: Prunes contain masses of pectin, a soluble fiber that accounts for their laxative effect. Pectin also helps lower blood cholesterol levels.

Strawberries: Rich in vitamin C and soluble and insoluble fiber that help remove cholesterol from the blood.

Asparagus: An excellent source of beta carotene and a useful source of vitamins C and E (all natural antioxidants that may help lower blood cholesterol).

Above: Eating plenty of fruit and vegetables nowadays is a treat, not a punishment!

Avocados: Rich in monounsaturates thought to limit damage caused to arteries by 'bad' LDL cholesterol. A good source of vitamin E—a powerful antioxidant—and may be included in a low-fat diet in moderation. Serve with a fat-free dressing.

Broccoli: Probably topping the list of disease-fighting vegetables, broccoli is an excellent source of antioxidants carotene, vitamins C and E and cholesterol-lowering soluble fiber.

Carrots: A fantastic source of beta carotene, a powerful antioxidant that protects the arteries from damage by 'bad' LDL cholesterol. Carrots are also very rich in cholesterol-lowering soluble fiber.

Garlic: An all-around miracle vegetable, widely believed to thin the blood and reduce blood cholesterol. Use raw in salad dressings, roast whole heads and eat with a selection of roasted vegetables, or sauté gently in stir-fries, sauces and stews.

Kale: A rich source of antioxidant vitamins, which help protect against 'bad' LDL cholesterol. Tender baby kale can be microwaved or used raw in salads.

Mushrooms: Sweat in a little stock rather than butter or slice and use raw in salads. Eaten daily, Asian mushrooms (shiitake) are thought to reduce blood cholesterol and high blood pressure.

Onions: Onions are an exceptionally powerful antioxidant and widely believed to thin the blood and lower cholesterol. An essential flavoring for many savory dishes; serve them cooked or raw in salads, or baked as a vegetable in their own right.

Parsnips: A tasty root vegetable rich in cholesterol-lowering soluble fiber. Eat baked, mashed or grated raw on top of salads.

Potatoes: Provide energy-giving carbohydrate, vitamin C and soluble fiber, but are frequently prepared using high-fat cooking methods such as roasting and frying. Boil, steam or bake potatoes instead, and serve with low-fat dressings.

Sweet peppers: An excellent source of beta carotene and vitamin C, which help reduce damage caused by 'bad' LDL cholesterol. Use raw in salads, add to stir-fries, roast in the oven and add to soups, stews and sauces.

COOKING WITH LOW-FAT AND FAT-FREE INGREDIENTS

Nowadays many foods are available in reduced-fat or very low-fat versions. In every supermarket you'll find a huge array of low-fat dairy products such as reduced-fat milk and cream, yogurt, hard and soft cheeses and fromage frais; reduced-fat cookies; reduced-fat or fat-free salad dressings and mayonnaise; reduced-fat chips and snacks, and low-fat, half-fat or very low-fat spreads, as well as reduced-fat ready-made meals.

Other foods, such as fresh fruit and vegetables, pasta, rice, potatoes and bread, naturally contain very little fat, and they help reduce cholesterol levels. Some food additions, such as soy sauce, wine, vinegar, cider, sherry and honey, contain no fat at all. By combining these and other low-fat foods you can create delicious dishes that contain very little fat.

Some low-fat or reduced-fat ingredients and products work better than others in cooking, but often a simple substitution of one for another will produce good results.

Some low-fat or reduced-fat ingredients and products work better than others in cooking, but often a simple substitution of one for another will produce good results.

LOW-FAT SPREADS IN COOKING

There is a huge variety of low-fat, reduced-fat and half-fat spreads available in supermarkets. Only some are suitable for cooking.

Generally speaking, the very low-fat spreads, with a fat content of around 20 percent or less, have a high water content and are therefore unsuitable for cooking.

Clockwise from left: olive oil, sunflower oil, buttermilk blend, sunflower light, olive oil reduced-fat spread, reduced-fat butter and (center) very low-fat spread.

Low-fat or half-fat spreads with a fat content of around 40 percent can be used for some cooking methods. They are suitable for use in one-bowl cake and cookie recipes, one-pot sauce recipes, sautéing vegetables over low heat, and making pâte à choux and some cake icings.

When these low-fat spreads are used for cooking, the fat may behave slightly differently from full-fat products such as butter or margarine. With some recipes, the cooked result may be slightly different from that produced by the traditional method but will still be acceptable. Other recipes will be just as tasty and successful, if slightly different in texture.

For example, pâte à choux made using half- or low-fat spread is often slightly crisper and lighter in texture than traditional pâte à choux, while a cheesecake crust made with melted half- or low-fat spread combined with crushed cookie crumbs, may be slightly softer in texture and less crispy than most crusts traditionally made using melted butter.

LOW-FAT AND VERY LOW-FAT SNACKS

Instead of reaching for chips, a high-fat cookie or a chocolate bar or cake when hunger strikes, try one of these delicious low-fat snacks instead.

● A piece of fresh fruit or vegetable such as an apple, banana or carrot is delicious and will also increase soluble fiber and help lower cholesterol. Keep chunks or sticks wrapped in a plastic bag in the refrigerator. If you like, skewer them on to cocktail sticks or short bamboo skewers to make them into mini kababs.

● Crackers, such as water biscuits or crisp breads, spread with reduced sugar jam or marmalade.

● Very low-fat plain or fruit yogurt or fromage frais.

● Snack on pitas, whole-wheat rolls or tortillas, or bake your own version, such as Saffron Foccacia.

● A bowl of whole-wheat breakfast cereal or no-added-sugar muesli served with a little skim milk. Oats are one of the best cereals for reducing cholesterol.

● A portion of canned fruit in natural fruit juice, served with a spoonful or two of fat-free yogurt.

● One or two rice cakes or oat cakes—delicious on their own, or topped with honey or reduced fat cheese. Oats are well known for their cholesterol-lowering properties.

● A handful of dried fruit such as raisins or apricots will help lower blood cholesterol levels. Dried fruit makes a perfect addition to children's (and adults!) packed lunches or snacks.

When heating half- or low-fat spreads, never cook them over high heat. Always use a heavy pan over low heat to avoid burning, spitting or curdling, and stir constantly. With one-pot sauces, the mixture should be whisked over low heat.

Half-fat or low-fat spreads are not suitable for shallow- or deep-fat frying, pastry making, rich fruitcakes, some cookies or in place of clarified butter and preserves. Remember that the keeping qualities of recipes made using half- or low-fat spreads may be reduced slightly, due to the lower fat content.

Another way to reduce the fat content of recipes, particularly cake recipes, is to use a dried fruit purée in place of all or some of the fat in a recipe. By using dried fruit, you'll also be increasing your intake of soluble fiber, which, in turn, helps reduce cholesterol levels. Many cake recipes work well using dried fruit purée, but other recipes may not be so successful. Pastry does not work well, for instance. Breads work very well—perhaps because the amount of fat is usually relatively small—as do some cookies and floury-based items, such as brownies and pancakes.

To make a dried fruit purée to use in recipes, chop 4 ounces ready-to-eat dried fruit, place in a blender or food processor with $^1/_3$ cup water and blend until almost puréed; the mixture should have some texture. Then, simply substitute the same weight of this dried fruit purée for all or just some of the amount of fat in the recipe. The purée will keep in the fridge for up to three days.

You can use prunes, dried apricots, dried peaches or dried apples, or substitute mashed fresh fruit, such as ripe bananas or lightly cooked apples, without the added water.

EASY WAYS TO CUT DOWN ON FAT

There are lots of simple, no-fuss ways of reducing fat in your daily diet. Just follow the simple 'eat less— try instead' suggestions to discover how easy it is.

Eat less—Butter, margarine and hard fats.

● *Try instead*—When baking chicken or fish, rather than adding a pat of butter, try wrapping the food in a loosely sealed parcel of foil, parchment or waxed paper and adding some wine or fruit juice and herbs or spices to the food before sealing the package.
● Where possible, use low- and very low-fat spreads, or non-hydrogenated vegetable margarine.

Eat less—Fatty meats and high-fat products such as meat pâtés, pies and sausages.

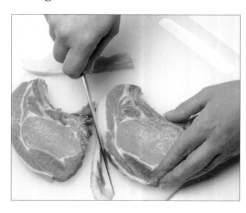

● *Try instead*—Low-fat meats such as chicken and turkey. Cut off any visible fat and skin before cooking.

● Eat fish more often. White fish is practically fat-free and oily fish contains essential cholesterol-lowering fatty acids.
● Make gravies using vegetable water or fat-free stock rather than using meat juices.

Eat less—Fried foods.
● *Try instead*—Fat-free cooking methods such as broiling, microwaving, steaming or baking whenever possible.
● When broiling foods, the addition of fat is often unnecessary. If the food shows signs of drying, you can lightly brush it with a small amount of monounsaturated oil such as olive or canola oil.
● Steaming or boiling are easy fat-free ways of cooking many foods, especially vegetables, fish and chicken.

● Try cooking in a nonstick wok with only a very small amount of oil.

Eat less—Hard cooking fats such as lard or hard margarine, and polyunsaturated oil such as corn, safflower and sunflower oils. These oils are easily oxidized and may cause 'bad' LDL cholesterol to become toxic.
● *Try instead*—Monounsaturated oils such as olive and canola oils. These protect the arteries by reducing 'bad' LDL cholesterol without lowering the level of 'good' HDL cholesterol.
● Microwaved foods rarely need the addition of fat, so add herbs or spices for extra flavor.

Eat less—Added fat in cooking.
● *Try instead*—To cook with little or no fat. Whenever possible, use heavy, good-quality nonstick pans, so that the food doesn't stick.
● Try using a small amount of nonstick spray cooking oil to control exactly how much fat you are using.

● Always roast or broil meat or poultry on a rack.
● If you use heavy, good-quality cookware, you'll find that the amount of fat needed for cooking foods can be kept to an absolute minimum. When making casseroles or meat sauces such as bolognese, dry-fry the meat to brown it and then drain off all the excess fat before adding the other ingredients. If you do need a little fat, choose an oil that is high in mono-unsaturates such as olive or canola oil, and always use as little as possible.

● Use fat-free or low-fat ingredients, such as fruit juice, low-fat or fat-free stock, wine or even beer for cooking.

● When serving vegetables such as boiled potatoes, carrots or peas, resist the temptation to add a pat of butter or margarine. Instead, sprinkle with chopped fresh herbs, freshly ground spices, lemon juice or soy sauce.

● Try poaching foods such as chicken, fish or fruit in stock or syrup.

● Sauté vegetables in wine, fruit juice or low-fat or fat-free stock.

● Marinate meat or poultry in wine, herbs or spices, and vinegar or fruit juice. This will help to tenderize the meat, as well as adding flavor and color. In addition, the marinade can be used for basting during cooking.

● Cook vegetables in a covered saucepan over a low heat with a little water, so they cook in their own juices.

● Try braising vegetables in the oven in wine, low-fat or fat-free stock, or even water with the addition of some herbs.

● Poach fruit in wine for a quick, low-fat dessert. Serve with a dollop of fresh yogurt instead of cream.

Eat less—Eggs, which are high in both saturated fat and cholesterol. Limit intake to no more than 3 or 4 a week.

● *Try instead*—Egg whites in recipes calling for whole eggs. Limit egg yolks to 1 per serving when making scrambled eggs. For something a little different, make mayonnaise with tofu instead of egg yolks.

Eat less—Rich creamy, salad dressings such as full-fat mayonnaise, French or Thousand Island.

● *Try instead*—Reduced-fat or fat-free mayonnaise or dressings. Make salad dressings at home with low-fat yogurt or fromage frais, and use blender-whipped cottage cheese, ricotta or buttermilk in recipes calling for sour cream or mayonnaise.

● Try lemon juice, soy sauce and fresh herbs on salads – quick and easy but also full of flavor.

Eat less—Full-fat dairy products such as whole milk, cream, butter, hard margarine, crème fraîche, whole-milk yogurts and hard cheese.

● *Try instead*—Semi-skim or skim milk and milk products, low-fat yogurts, low-fat fromage frais and low- and reduced-fat cheeses, and reduced-fat creams and crème fraîche.

● Beware of dried skim milk and coffee creamers – these may be skimmed of animal fat, but may have vegetable fat added.

Eat less—High-fat snacks such as potato chips, tortilla chips, fried snacks and pastries, chocolate cakes, muffins, doughnuts, sweet pastries and cookies—especially chocolate ones!

● *Try instead*—Low-fat and fat-free fresh or dried fruits, breadsticks or vegetable sticks.

● Make your own low-fat cakes and baked goods.

● Look out for nonstick coated fabric sheet. This reusable nonstick material is amazingly versatile; it can be cut to size and used to line cake pans, baking sheets or frying pans. Heat-resistant up to 550°F and microwave safe, it will last for up to five years.

● If you do buy ready-made cakes and cookies, always choose low-fat and reduced-fat versions.

● Use high-quality bakeware that doesn't need greasing before use.

● Use nonstick baking parchment paper and only lightly grease bakeware before lining.

HOW TO REDUCE OIL IN COOKING

For fat-free or low-fat cooking it's best to avoid roasting and frying, both of which can increase the fat content of food. Choose instead to poach, broil, bake, steam or microwave; all successful ways of cooking without adding fat. Below are some further techniques that may be used for reducing or eliminating the amount of oil used in cooking.

SWEATING VEGETABLES

GOOD FOR: Pan-frying vegetables such as onions, mushrooms, carrots and celery, which would usually be initially fried in oil or butter, as the basis of many savory recipes.

HOW TO: Put the sliced vegetables into a nonstick frying pan with about ²/₃ cup low-fat stock. Cook for 5 minutes or until the vegetables are tender and the stock has reduced. Add 1 tablespoon dry wine or wine vinegar for a little piquancy and continue cooking for a further few minutes until the vegetables are lightly browned.

MARINATING

GOOD FOR: Adding flavor as well as helping to tenderize and keep the food moist during cooking without adding any fat. Useful for meat, fish, poultry and vegetables. The marinade may also be used for basting or it can be added to an accompanying sauce.

HOW TO: Wine, soy sauce, vinegar, citrus juices and yogurt all make excellent fat-free marinade bases with herbs and spices added for extra flavor. Leave fish for 1 hour, marinate meat and poultry overnight if possible.

PARCEL COOKING

GOOD FOR: Fish, chicken, vegetables and fruit, allowing the food to cook in its own juices and the steam created, holding in all the flavor and nutrient value and eliminating the need for oil or fats.

HOW TO: Enclose food in individual foil, parchments, or waxed paper packages, add extra flavorings, such as a little wine, herbs and spices, if desired. Twist or fold ends to secure and ensure that the juices can't run out, then either bake, steam or, if using foil, cook on a grill.

SEARING

GOOD FOR: Sealing the juices into meat and poultry. Even lean cuts trimmed of skin and visible fat contain some hidden fat, so adding extra fat isn't necessary.

HOW TO: Place the meat in a heavy pan over moderate heat and brown evenly on all sides. If the meat sticks slightly, remove from the pan, brush or spray a little olive oil onto the pan's surface, heat, then return the meat to the pan. Drain off any excess fat that comes out of the meat.

LOW-FAT SAUCES

Sauces can introduce an unwelcome amount of fat into a recipe so that naturally low-fat foods like vegetables, white fish and skinless chicken may end up being served in a rich, high-fat coating. However, by following the tips and techniques below, it's easy to adapt such sauces without sacrificing flavor and appeal.

BÉARNAISE SAUCE

Some fat savings can be made to this classic piquant sauce by using a small amount of butter and fewer egg yolks.

INGREDIENTS

Makes 1½ cups
⅓ cup white wine
4 tablespoons white wine vinegar
1 tablespoon finely chopped shallot
1 tablespoon cornstarch
¼ cup water
2 egg yolks, lightly beaten
3 tablespoons unsalted butter, melted
1 tablespoon chopped fresh tarragon
1 tablespoon chopped fresh parsley
salt and black pepper

1 Put the wine, vinegar, shallot and freshly ground black pepper in a saucepan. Bring to a boil and simmer until reduced to 2–3 tablespoons. Strain, discarding solids.

2 Put the cornstarch and water in a bowl over a pan of gently simmering water. Whisk for 3–4 minutes until thickened. Stir in the vinegar mixture. Remove from the heat, whisk in the egg yolks and half the butter. Place over the hot water again and stir constantly for 3–4 minutes until thickened.

3 Add the chopped herbs. Whisk in the remaining butter and salt to taste. Use immediately.

EGG-FREE MAYONNAISE

Egg yolks are high in cholesterol and contain saturated fat. Here's a way of making mayonnaise without them.

INGREDIENTS

Makes 1 cup
4 ounces firm tofu, drained and pressed dry
4 tablespoons low-fat plain yogurt or fromage frais
2 tablespoons white wine or cider vinegar
1 teaspoon sea salt
5 tablespoons olive oil
black pepper

Put the tofu, yogurt or fromage frais, wine or vinegar and salt in a blender and process for 2–3 minutes until very smooth. With the blender running, add the oil a little at a time, until the mixture thickens. Season. Use immediately.

OIL-FREE DRESSINGS

Whisk together 6 tablespoons low-fat plain yogurt and 2 tablespoons lemon juice and season to taste with freshly ground black pepper. If you prefer, wine, cider or fruit vinegar or even orange juice could be used in place of the lemon juice. Add chopped fresh herbs, crushed garlic, mustard, honey, or other flavorings, if you like.

VEGETABLE PURÉE

Many recipes for sauces are traditionally thickened by adding cream, beurre manié (a butter and flour paste) or egg yolks, all of which add saturated fat and cholesterol to the sauce. If cooked vegetables are included in the recipe, blend some down in a food processor to make a purée, then stir back into the juices to produce a thickened sauce.

THREE WAYS TO MAKE LOW-FAT SAUCES

The traditional roux method for making a sauce won't work successfully if using a low-fat spread. This is because of the high water content, which will evaporate on heating, leaving insufficient fat to blend with the flour. However, below are three quick and easy low-fat alternatives.

1 The one-pot method: Place 2 tablespoons each of low-fat spread and all-purpose flour in a heavy, good-quality pan with 1¼ cups skim milk. Bring to a boil, whisking continuously until thickened and smooth.

2 Using stock to replace fat: Sweat cut-up vegetables, such as onions and mushrooms, in a small amount of stock in a nonstick pan rather than frying in fat.

3 Using cornstarch to thicken: Blend 1 tablespoon cornstarch with 1–2 tablespoons cold water, then whisk into 1¼ cups simmering stock or milk, bring to a boil and cook for a further 1 minute, stirring continuously.

LOW-FAT STOCKS

A good stock is invaluable in the kitchen. The most delicious soups, stews, casseroles and sauces rely on a good home-made stock for success. Neither a stock cube nor a canned consommé will do if you want the best flavor.

Simple and economical to make, below are three easy-to-follow recipes for low-fat chicken, meat and vegetable stock. Keep in the refrigerator for 4 days, or freeze for up to 6 months for meat and poultry, 1 month for the vegetable.

LOW-FAT CHICKEN STOCK

INGREDIENTS

Makes about 6 cups
2¼ *pounds chicken wings or thighs,*
  skinned
1 *onion*
2 *whole garlic cloves*
1 *bay leaf*
1 *thyme sprig*
3–4 *parsley sprigs*
10 *black peppercorns*

1 Cut the chicken into pieces and put into a large, heavy saucepan. Peel the onion and stud with the cloves. Tie the bay leaf, thyme, parsley and peppercorns in a piece of cheesecloth and add to the saucepan together with the onion.

2 Pour in 7½ cups of cold water. Slowly bring to simmering point, skimming off any scum that rises to the surface with a slotted spoon. Continue to simmer very gently, uncovered, for 1½ hours.

3 Strain the stock through a sieve into a large bowl and let sit until cold, then chill. Remove solidified fat from the surface. Keep chilled in the refrigerator for up to 4 days, or freeze in usable amounts.

LOW-FAT MEAT STOCK

INGREDIENTS

Makes about 9 cups
4 *pounds lean veal bones, trimmed*
2 *onions, unpeeled, quartered*
2 *carrots, roughly chopped*
2 *celery stalks, with leaves if possible,*
  roughly chopped
2 *tomatoes, coarsely chopped*
a handful of parsley stalks
a few fresh thyme sprigs or
  ¾ teaspoon dried thyme
2 *bay leaves*
10 *black peppercorns, lightly crushed*

1 Put the bones and vegetables in a large stockpot. Add 7½ pints of cold water. Bring just to a boil, skimming to remove all the foam from the surface. Add the parsley, thyme, bay leaves and peppercorns.

2 Partly cover the pot and simmer the stock for 4–6 hours. The bones and vegetables should always be covered with liquid, so top up with a little boiling water from time to time.

3 Strain the stock through a sieve. Skim as much fat as possible from the surface. If possible, cool the stock and then refrigerate it; the fat will rise to the top and set in a layer that can be removed easily.

VEGETABLE STOCK

INGREDIENTS

Makes about 6 cups
2 *carrots*
2 *celery sticks*
2 *onions*
2 *tomatoes*
10 *mushroom stems*
2 *bay leaves*
1 *thyme sprig*
3–4 *parsley sprigs*
10 *black peppercorns*

1 Roughly chop the carrots, celery sticks, onions, tomatoes and mushroom stems. Place them in a large, heavy saucepan. Tie the bay leaves, thyme, parsley and peppercorns in a piece of cheesecloth and add to the pan.

2 Pour in 7½ cups cold water. Slowly bring to simmering point. Continue to simmer very gently, uncovered, for 1½ hours.

3 Strain through a sieve into a large bowl and let sit until cool. Keep chilled in the refrigerator for up to 4 days, or freeze in usable amounts.

LOW-FAT SWEET OPTIONS

Desserts needn't be banned from a low-fat, low cholesterol diet. Many traditional dairy products, such as cream are high in fat, but it's a simple matter to adapt recipes and use low-fat alternatives to create delicious results.

Low-fat yogurt (vanilla is particularly delicious for desserts), fromage frais and reduced-fat crème fraîche may be substituted for cream and skim milk can be used in sauces, but here are some further simple ideas to try.

LOW-FAT CREAMY WHIP

A sweetened cream that can be used in place of whipped real dairy cream. It isn't suitable for cooking, but freezes very well.

INGREDIENTS

Makes ²/₃ cup
½ teaspoon powdered gelatin
¼ cup skim-milk powder
1 tablespoon superfine sugar
1 tablespoon lemon juice

1 Sprinkle the gelatin over 1 tablespoon cold water in a small bowl and leave to 'sponge' for 5 minutes. Place the bowl over a saucepan of hot water and stir until dissolved. Leave to cool.

2 Whisk the skim-milk powder, superfine sugar, lemon juice and 4 tablespoons cold water until frothy. Add the dissolved gelatin and whisk for a few seconds more. Chill in the refrigerator for 30 minutes.

3 Whisk the chilled mixture again until very thick and frothy. Serve within 30 minutes of making.

YOGURT PIPING CREAM

An excellent alternative to traditional whipped real dairy cream for decorating cakes and desserts.

INGREDIENTS

Makes about 2 cups
2 teaspoons powdered gelatin
1¼ cups strained yogurt
 (see right)
1 tablespoon sugar
½ teaspoon vanilla extract
1 egg white

1 Sprinkle the gelatin over 3 tablespoons cold water in a small bowl and leave to 'sponge' for 5 minutes. Place the bowl over a saucepan of hot water and stir until dissolved. Leave to cool.

2 Mix together the yogurt, sugar and vanilla extract. Stir in the gelatin. Chill in the refrigerator for 30 minutes, or until just beginning to set around the edges.

3 Whisk the egg white until stiff and carefully fold it into the yogurt mixture. Spoon into a piping bag fitted with a nozzle and use immediately.

STRAINED YOGURT AND SIMPLE CURD CHEESE

Strained yogurt is simple to make and lower in fat than many commercial varieties. Serve with puddings, instead of cream. Simple curd cheese can be used instead of sour cream, cream cheese or butter, flavored accordingly for sweet or savory recipes.

INGREDIENTS

Makes 1¼ cups yogurt or ½ cup curd cheese
2½ cups natural low-fat yogurt

1 For strained yogurt, line a nylon or stainless-steel sieve with a double layer of cheesecloth. Put over a bowl and pour in the yogurt.

2 Leave to drain in the refrigerator for 3 hours—the mixture will have separated into thick strained yogurt and watery whey. If desired, sweeten with a little honey.

3 To make simple curd cheese, follow step 1 above, then leave to drain in the refrigerator for 8 hours or overnight. Spoon the resulting curd cheese into a bowl, cover and keep chilled until required.

THE FAT AND CALORIE CONTENT OF FOOD

The following figures show the weight of fat (g) and the energy content per 4 ounces of each food.

VEGETABLES

	FAT (g)	SAT. FAT (g)	CHOL (mg)	ENERGY		FAT (g)	SAT. FAT (g)	CHOL (mg)	ENERGY
Broccoli	0.9	0.2	0	33 Kcals/138 kJ	Peas	1.5	0.3	0	83 Kcals/344 kJ
Cabbage	0.4	0.1	0	26 Kcals/109 kJ	Potatoes	0.2	trace	0	75 Kcals/318 kJ
Carrots	0.3	0.1	0	35 Kcals/146 kJ	Fries, home-made in dripping	6.7	3.7	6	189 Kcals/796 kJ
Cauliflower	0.9	0.2	0	34 Kcals/142 kJ	Fries, retail (in blended oil)	12.4	1.1	0	239 Kcals/1001 kJ
Cucumber	0.1	trace	0	10 Kcals/40 kJ	Oven-chips, frozen, baked	4.2	1.8	0	162 Kcals/687 kJ
Mushrooms	0.5	0.1	0	13 Kcals/55 kJ	Tomatoes	0.3	0.1	0	17 Kcals/73 kJ
Onions	0.2	trace	0	36 Kcals/151 kJ	Zucchini	0.4	0.1	0	18 Kcals/74 kJ

BEANS AND PULSES

	FAT (g)	SAT. FAT (g)	CHOL (mg)	ENERGY		FAT (g)	SAT. FAT (g)	CHOL (mg)	ENERGY
Black-eyed peas, cooked	0.7	0.5	0	116 Kcals/494 kJ	Lima beans, canned	0.5	0.1	0	77 Kcals/327 kJ
Chickpeas, canned	2.9	0.3	0	115 Kcals/487 kJ	Red kidney beans, canned	0.6	0.1	0	100 Kcals/424 kJ
Hummus	12.6	n/a	0	187 Kcals/781 kJ	Red lentils, cooked	0.4	trace	0	100 Kcals/424 kJ

FISH AND SEAFOOD

	FAT (g)	SAT. FAT (g)	CHOL (mg)	ENERGY		FAT (g)	SAT. FAT (g)	CHOL (mg)	ENERGY
Cod fillets, fresh	0.7	0.1	46	80 Kcals/337 kJ	Roe, cod's, fried	11.9	1.2	500	202 Kcals/861 kJ
Crab, canned	0.5	0.1	72	77 Kcals/326 kJ	Shrimp	0.9	0.2	280	99 Kcals/418 kJ
Haddock, fresh	0.6	0.1	36	81 Kcals/345 kJ	Trout, grilled	5.4	1.1	70	135 Kcals/565 kJ
Lemon sole, fresh	1.5	0.2	60	83 Kcals/351 kJ	Tuna, canned in water	0.6	1.4	50	99 Kcals/422 kJ

MEAT AND MEAT PRODUCTS

	FAT (g)	SAT. FAT (g)	CHOL (mg)	ENERGY		FAT (g)	SAT. FAT (g)	CHOL (mg)	ENERGY
Bacon rasher, streaky, raw	23.6	8.2	65	276 Kcals/1142 kJ	Lamb chops, loin, lean and fat	23.0	10.8	79	277 Kcals/1150 kJ
Beef ground, extra lean, raw	9.6	4.2	56	174 Kcals/728 kJ	Liver, lamb, raw	6.2	1.7	430	137 Kcals/575 kJ
Beef ground, raw	16.2	7.1	60	225 Kcals/934 kJ	Pork, average, lean, raw	4.0	1.4	63	123 Kcals/519 kJ
Chicken fillet, raw	1.1	0.3	70	106 Kcals/449 kJ	Pork chops, loin, lean and fat	21.7	8.0	61	270 Kcals/1119 kJ
Chicken, roasted, meat and skin	12.5	3.4	110	218 Kcals/910 kJ	Rump steak, lean and marbled	10.1	4.3	60	174 Kcals/726 kJ
Duck, meat only, raw	6.5	2.0	110	137 Kcals/575 kJ	Rump steak, lean only	4.1	1.7	59	125 Kcals/526 kJ
Duck, roasted, meat, fat and skin	38.1	11.4	99	423 Kcals/1750 kJ	Salami	45.2	n/a	n/a	491 Kcals/2031 kJ
Ham, premium	5.0	1.7	58	132 Kcals/553 kJ	Sausage roll, flaky pastry	36.4	13.4	49	477 Kcals/1985 kJ
Lamb, average, lean, raw	8.3	3.8	74	156 Kcals/651 kJ	Turkey, meat only, raw	1.6	0.5	70	105 Kcals/443 kJ

Information from *The Composition of Foods* (5th edition 1991) is reproduced with the permission of the Royal Society of Chemistry and the Controller of Her Majesty's Stationery Office.

DAIRY, FATS AND OILS

	FAT (g)	SAT. FAT (g)	CHOL (mg)	ENERGY		FAT (g)	SAT. FAT (g)	CHOL (mg)	ENERGY
Brie	26.9	16.8	100	319 Kcals/1323 kJ	Fromage frais, plain	7.1	4.4	25	113 Kcals/469 kJ
Butter	81.7	54	230	737 Kcals/3031 kJ	Fromage frais, very low-fat	0.2	0.1	1	58 Kcals/247 kJ
Cream, heavy	48.0	30	130	449 Kcals/1849 kJ	Greek yogurt	9.1	5.2	n/a	115 Kcals/477 kJ
Cream, light	19.1	11.9	55	198 Kcals/817 kJ	Greek yogurt, reduced-fat	5.0	3.1	13	80 Kcals/335 kJ
Cream, whipping	39.3	24.6	105	373 Kcals/1539 kJ	Low-fat spread	40.5	11.2	6	390 Kcals/1605 kJ
Crème fraîche	40.0	25	105	379 Kcals/1567 kJ	Low-fat spread, extra	25	6.5	n/a	273 Kcals/1128 kJ
Crème fraîche, reduced fat	15.0	9.4	n/a	165 Kcals/683 kJ	Low-fat yogurt, plain	0.8	0.5	4	56 Kcals/236 kJ
Cheddar cheese	34.4	21.7	100	412 Kcals/1708 kJ	Margarine, polyunsaturated	81.6	16.2	7	739 Kcals/3039 kJ
Cheddar-type, reduced-fat	15.0	9.4	43	261 Kcals/1091 kJ	Mayonnaise	75.6	11.1	75	691 Kcals/2843 kJ
Corn oil	99.9	12.7	0	899 Kcals/3696 kJ	Mayonnaise, reduced calorie	28.1	4.5	n/a	288 Kcals/1188 kJ
Cream cheese	47.4	29.7	95	439 Kcals/1807 kJ	Milk, semi-skim	1.6	1.0	7	46 Kcals/195 kJ
Edam cheese	25.4	15.9	80	333 Kcals/1382 kJ	Milk, skim	0.1	0.1	2	33 Kcals/130 kJ
Egg, whole	10.8	3.1	385	147 Kcals/612 kJ	Milk, whole	3.9	2.4	14	66 Kcals/275 kJ
Egg white	trace	trace	trace	36 Kcals/153 kJ	Olive oil	99.9	14	0	899 Kcals/3696 kJ
Egg yolk	30.5	8.7	1120	339 Kcals/1402 kJ	Parmesan cheese	32.7	20.5	100	452 Kcals/1880 kJ
Fat-free dressing	1.2	0	0	67 Kcals/282 kJ	Safflower oil	99.9	10.2	0	899 Kcals/3696 kJ
Feta cheese	20.2	13.7	70	250 Kcals/1037 kJ	Shortening	99.0	40.8	93	891 Kcals/3663 kJ
French dressing	49.4	10	0	462 Kcals/1902 kJ	Skim milk soft cheese	trace	trace	1	74 Kcals/313 kJ

CEREALS, BAKING AND PRESERVES

	FAT (g)	SAT. FAT (g)	CHOL (mg)	ENERGY		FAT (g)	SAT. FAT (g)	CHOL (mg)	ENERGY
Bread, brown	2.0	0.4	0	218 Kcals/927 kJ	Honey	0	0	0	288 Kcals/1229 kJ
Bread, white	1.9	0.4	0	235 Kcals/1002 kJ	Lemon curd, home-made	0.8	0.3	150	176 Kcals/736 kJ
Bread, whole-wheat	2.5	0.5	0	215 Kcals/914 kJ	Pasta, white, uncooked	1.8	0.2	0	342 Kcals/1456 kJ
Chocolate, semisweet	29.2	16.9	9	510 Kcals/2157 kJ	Pasta, whole-wheat, uncooked	2.5	0.4	0	324 Kcals/1379 kJ
Chocolate, sweet	30.3	17.8	30	520 Kcals/2214 kJ	Raisin bran	1.6	0.4	0	303 Kcals/1289 kJ
Cornflakes	0.7	0.1	0	360 Kcals/1535 kJ	Rice, brown, uncooked	2.8	0.7	0	357 Kcals/1518 kJ
Croissant	20.3	6.5	75	360 Kcals/1505 kJ	Rice, white, uncooked	3.6	0.9	0	383 Kcals/1630 kJ
Digestive biscuit (plain)	20.9	8.6	41	471 Kcals/1978 kJ	Shortbread	26.1	17.3	74	498 Kcals/2087 kJ
Doughnut, jelly	14.5	4.3	15	336 Kcals/1414 kJ	Spongecake	16.9	8.8	n/a	393 Kcals/1652 kJ
Flapjack	26.6	7.6	43	484 Kcals/2028 kJ	Spongecake, fatless	6.1	1.7	223	294 Kcals/1245 kJ
Fruit cake, rich	11	3.4	63	341 Kcals/1438 kJ	Sugar, white	0	0	0	105 Kcals/394 kJ
Fruit jam	0	0	0	261 Kcals/1116 kJ	Swiss-style granola	5.9	0.8	trace	363 Kcals/1540 kJ

FRUIT AND NUTS

	FAT (g)	SAT. FAT (g)	CHOL (mg)	ENERGY		FAT (g)	SAT. FAT (g)	CHOL (mg)	ENERGY
Almonds	55.8	4.7	0	612 Kcals/2534 kJ	Hazelnuts	63.5	4.7	0	650 Kcals/2685 kJ
Apples	0.1	trace	0	47 Kcals/199 kJ	Oranges	0.1	trace	0	37 Kcals/158 kJ
Avocados	19.5	4.1	0	190 Kcals/784 kJ	Peaches	0.1	trace	0	33 Kcals/142 kJ
Bananas	0.3	0.1	0	95 Kcals/403 kJ	Peanut butter, smooth	53.7	11.7	0	623 Kcals/2581 kJ
Brazil nuts	68.2	16.4	0	682 Kcals/2813 kJ	Pears	0.1	trace	0	40 Kcals/169 kJ
Dried mixed fruit	0.4	n/a	0	268 Kcals/1114 kJ	Pine nuts	68.6	4.6	0	688 Kcals/2840 kJ
Grapefruit	0.1	trace	0	30 Kcals/126 kJ	Walnuts	68.5	5.6	0	688 Kcals/2837 kJ

APPETIZERS AND SNACKS

For a healthy diet it makes good sense to include some homemade soups in everyday meals, packed with the goodness of fresh ingredients and very low in fat. As a light lunch with crusty whole-wheat bread, or as an appetizer, modern soups are extremely quick and easy to make. An added bonus is the wonderful variety of fresh, seasonal vegetables available all year so that soups, such as Mushroom, Celery and Garlic Soup and Red Bell Pepper Soup with Lime, can be enjoyed all year round. Other appetizers can double up as a light meal or snack; try Cucumber and Alfalfa Tortillas, and Lemony Stuffed Zucchini.

Cauliflower and Walnut Cream

Even though there's no cream added to this soup, the cauliflower gives it a delicious, rich, creamy texture.

──── INGREDIENTS ────

Serves 4
1 medium cauliflower
1 medium onion, coarsely chopped
1⅞ cups chicken or vegetable
   broth
1⅞ cups skim milk
3 tbsp walnut pieces
salt and black pepper
paprika and chopped walnuts, to
   garnish

1 Trim the cauliflower of outer leaves and break into small florets. Place the cauliflower, onion, and broth in a large saucepan.

2 Bring to a boil, cover, and simmer for about 15 minutes, or until soft. Add the milk and walnuts, then purée in a food processor until smooth.

3 Season the soup to taste, then bring to a boil. Serve sprinkled with paprika and chopped walnuts.

──── NUTRITION NOTES ────

Per portion:
Energy	166Kcals/699kJ
Fat	9.02g
Saturated fat	0.88g
Cholesterol	2.25mg
Fiber	2.73g

Curried Carrot and Apple Soup

──── INGREDIENTS ────

Serves 4
2 tsp sunflower oil
1 tbsp mild curry powder
1¼ lb carrots, chopped
1 large onion, chopped
1 tart baking apple, chopped
3⅔ cups chicken broth
salt and black pepper
plain low fat yogurt and carrot curls, to
   garnish

──── NUTRITION NOTES ────

Per portion:
Energy	114Kcals/477kJ
Fat	3.57g
Saturated fat	0.43g
Cholesterol	0.4mg
Fiber	4.99g

1 Heat the oil and gently fry the curry powder for 2–3 minutes.

2 Add the carrots, onion, and apple, stir well, then cover the pan.

3 Cook over very low heat for about 15 minutes, shaking the pan occasionally until softened. Spoon the vegetable mixture into a food processor or blender, then add half the broth and process until smooth.

4 Return to the pan and pour in the remaining broth. Bring the soup to a boil and adjust the seasoning before serving in bowls, garnished with a swirl of yogurt and a few curls of carrot.

TOMATO AND CILANTRO SOUP

This delicious soup is an ideal solution when time is short but you still want to produce a very stylish appetizer.

INGREDIENTS

Serves 4

1½lb small fresh tomatoes
2 tbsp vegetable oil
1 bay leaf
4 scallions, cut into
   1in pieces
1 tsp salt
1 garlic clove, crushed
1 tsp crushed black
   peppercorns
2 tbsp chopped fresh cilantro
3 cups water
1 tbsp cornstarch
4 tbsp single cream,
   to garnish

1 To skin the tomatoes, plunge them into very hot water for 30 seconds, then transfer to a bowl of cold water. The skin should now peel off quickly and easily. Chop the tomatoes into large chunks.

2 Heat the oil in a large saucepan, add the bay leaf and scallions, then stir in the tomatoes. Cook, stirring for a few more minutes until the tomatoes are softened.

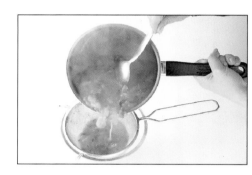

3 Add the salt, garlic, peppercorns, cilantro and water, bring to a boil, then simmer for 15 minutes.

4 Dissolve the cornstarch in a little water, remove the soup from the heat and press through a strainer.

5 Return the soup to the pan, add the cornstarch mixture and stir over a gentle heat until boiling and thickened.

6 Ladle the soup into shallow soup plates, then swirl a tablespoon of cream into each bowl before serving.

NUTRITION NOTES

Per portion:

Energy	129Kcals/474kJ
Fat	9.0g
Saturated fat	2.51g
Cholesterol	8.3mg
Fiber	1.9g

RED BELL PEPPER SOUP WITH LIME

The beautiful rich red color of this soup makes it a very attractive appetizer or light lunch. For a special dinner, toast some tiny croutons and serve sprinkled into the soup.

INGREDIENTS

Serves 4–6

4 red bell peppers, seeded and chopped
1 large onion, chopped
1 tsp olive oil
1 garlic clove, crushed
1 small red chili, sliced
3 tbsp tomato paste
3¾ cups chicken broth
finely grated rind and juice of 1 lime
salt and black pepper
shreds of lime rind, to garnish

1 Cook the onion and bell peppers gently in the oil in a covered saucepan for about 5 minutes, shaking the pan occasionally, until softened.

2 Stir in the garlic, then add the chili with the tomato paste. Stir in half the broth, then bring to a boil. Cover the pan and simmer for 10 minutes.

3 Cool slightly, then purée in a food processor or blender. Return to the pan, then add the remaining broth, the lime rind and juice, and seasoning.

4 Bring the soup back to a boil, then serve at once with a few strips of lime rind, scattered into each bowl.

NUTRITION NOTES	
Per portion:	
Energy	87Kcals/366kJ
Fat	1.57g
Saturated fat	0.12g
Cholesterol	0
Fiber	3.40g

MEDITERRANEAN TOMATO SOUP

Children will love this soup – especially if you use fancy shapes of pasta such as alphabet or animal shapes.

INGREDIENTS

Serves 4

1½ lb ripe plum tomatoes
1 medium onion, quartered
1 celery stalk
1 garlic clove
1 tbsp olive oil
1⅞ cups chicken broth
2 tbsp tomato paste
½ cup small pasta shapes
salt and black pepper
fresh cilantro or parsley, to garnish

1 Place the tomatoes, onion, celery, and garlic in a pan with the oil. Cover and cook over low heat for 40–45 minutes, shaking the pan occasionally, until very soft.

2 Spoon the vegetables into a food processor or blender and process until smooth. Press through a strainer, then return to the pan.

3 Stir in the broth and tomato paste and bring to a boil. Add the pasta and simmer gently for about 8 minutes, or until the pasta is tender. Add salt and pepper to taste, then sprinkle with cilantro or parsley and serve hot.

NUTRITION NOTES

Per portion:

Energy	112Kcals/474kJ
Fat	3.61g
Saturated fat	0.49g
Cholesterol	0
Fiber	2.68g

MUSHROOM, CELERY, AND GARLIC SOUP

INGREDIENTS

Serves 4

3 cups chopped mushrooms
4 celery stalks, chopped
3 garlic cloves
3 tbsp dry sherry or white wine
3⅔ cups chicken broth
2 tbsp Worcestershire sauce
1 tsp ground nutmeg
salt and black pepper
celery leaves, to garnish

NUTRITION NOTES

Per portion:

Energy	48Kcals/200kJ
Fat	1.09g
Saturated fat	0.11g
Cholesterol	0
Fiber	1.64g

1 Place the mushrooms, celery, and garlic in a pan and stir in the sherry or wine. Cover and cook over low heat for 30–40 minutes, until tender.

2 Add half the broth and purée in a food processor or blender until smooth. Return to the pan and add the remaining broth, the Worcestershire sauce, and nutmeg.

3 Bring to a boil, season, and serve hot, garnished with celery leaves.

Mushroom Croustades

The rich mushroom flavor of this filling is heightened by the addition of Worcestershire sauce.

Ingredients

Serves 2–4
1 short baguette, about 25cm/10in
2 tsp olive oil
9oz open cup mushrooms, quartered
2 tsp Worcestershire sauce
2 tsp lemon juice
2 tbsp skim milk
2 tbsp snipped fresh chives
salt and black pepper
snipped fresh chives, to garnish

1 Preheat the oven to 400°F. Cut the baguette in half lengthwise. Cut a scoop out of the soft middle of each using a sharp knife, leaving a thick border all the way around.

2 Brush the bread with oil, place on a baking sheet, and bake for about 6–8 minutes, until golden and crisp.

3 Place the mushrooms in a small saucepan with the Worcestershire sauce, lemon juice, and milk. Simmer for about 5 minutes, or until most of the liquid is evaporated.

4 Remove from the heat, then add the chives and seasoning. Spoon into the bread croustades and serve hot, garnished with snipped chives.

Nutrition Notes

Per portion:
Energy	324Kcals/1361kJ
Fat	6.4g
Saturated fat	1.27g
Cholesterol	0.3mg
Fiber	3.07g

CUCUMBER AND ALFALFA TORTILLAS

Wheat tortillas are extremely simple to prepare at home. Served with a crisp, fresh salsa, they make a marvelous appetizer, light lunch or supper dish.

INGREDIENTS

Serves 4
2 cups flour, sifted
pinch of salt
3 tbsp olive oil
½–⅔ cup warm water
lime wedges, to garnish

For the salsa
1 red onion, finely chopped
1 red chili, seeded and
    finely chopped
2 tbsp chopped fresh dill
    or cilantro
½ cucumber, peeled and chopped
2 cups alfalfa sprouts

For the sauce
1 large ripe avocado, peeled
    and pitted
juice of 1 lime
2 tbsp soft goat cheese
pinch of paprika

1 Mix all the salsa ingredients together in a bowl and set aside.

2 For the sauce, place the avocado, lime juice and goat cheese in a food processor or blender and process until smooth. Place in a bowl and cover with plastic wrap. Dust with paprika just before serving.

3 For the tortillas, place the flour and salt in a food processor or blender, add the oil and process. Gradually add the water until a stiff dough has formed. Turn out on to a floured board and knead until smooth.

4 Divide the mixture into eight pieces. Knead each piece for a couple of minutes and form into a ball. Flatten and roll out each ball to a 9in round.

NUTRITION NOTES

Per portion:
Energy	395Kcals/1659kJ
Fat	20.17g
Saturated fat	1.69g
Cholesterol	4.38mg
Fiber	4.15g

5 Heat a nonstick or ungreased heavy-based pan. Cook one tortilla at a time for about 30 seconds on each side. Place the cooked tortillas in a clean dish towel and repeat until you have made eight tortillas.

6 Spread each tortilla with a spoonful of avocado sauce, top with the salsa and roll up. Serve garnished with lime wedges and eat immediately.

> **COOK'S TIP**
> When peeling the avocado be sure to scrape off the bright green flesh from immediately under the skin as this gives the sauce its vivid green color.

CHEESE AND SPINACH PUFFS

— INGREDIENTS —

Serves 6

1 cup cooked, chopped spinach
¾ cup cottage cheese
1 tsp ground nutmeg
2 egg whites
2 tbsp grated Parmesan cheese
salt and black pepper

1 Preheat the oven to 425°F. Brush six ramekin dishes with oil.

2 Mix together the spinach and cottage cheese in a small bowl, then add the nutmeg and seasoning to taste.

3 Whisk the egg whites in a separate bowl until stiff enough to hold soft peaks. Fold them evenly into the spinach mixture using a spatula or large metal spoon, then spoon the mixture into the oiled ramekins, dividing it evenly, and smooth the tops.

4 Sprinkle with the Parmesan and place on a baking sheet. Bake for 15–20 minutes, or until puffed and golden brown. Serve immediately.

— NUTRITION NOTES —

Per portion:	
Energy	47Kcals/195kJ
Fat	1.32g
Saturated fat	0.52g
Cholesterol	2.79mg
Fiber	0.53g

LEMONY STUFFED ZUCCHINI

— INGREDIENTS —

Serves 4

4 zucchini, about 6oz each
1 tsp sunflower oil
1 garlic clove, crushed
1 tsp ground lemongrass
finely grated rind and juice of ½ lemon
scant ¾ cup cooked long-grain rice
6oz cherry tomatoes, halved
2 tbsp toasted cashews
salt and black pepper
sprigs of thyme, to garnish

— NUTRITION NOTES —

Per portion:	
Energy	126Kcals/530kJ
Fat	5.33g
Saturated fat	0.65g
Cholesterol	0
Fiber	2.31g

1 Preheat the oven to 400°F. Halve the zucchini lengthwise and use a teaspoon to scoop out the centers. Blanch the shells in boiling water for 1 minute, then drain well.

2 Chop the zucchini flesh finely and place in a saucepan with the oil and garlic. Stir over moderate heat until softened, but not browned.

3 Stir in the lemongrass, lemon rind and juice, rice, tomatoes, and cashews. Season well and spoon into the zucchini shells. Place the shells in a baking pan and cover with foil.

4 Bake for 25–30 minutes or until the zucchini is tender, then serve hot, garnished with thyme sprigs.

PASTA, PIZZAS, PULSES AND GRAINS

Pasta, pizzas, pulses and grain dishes should be encouraged at family meals as they're very healthy foods. They contain good amounts of protein, carbohydrates and vitamins, and are versatile and are usually low in fat. The recipes in this section provide lots of ideas for using these ingredients in tasty and exciting new ways. Add variety to meals by introducing different grains, such as polenta and couscous—they are just as healthy as rice and pasta, and just as delicious—try Baked Polenta with Tomatoes and Sweet Vegetable Couscous.

SPINACH AND HAZELNUT LASAGNE

A vegetarian dish that is hearty enough to satisfy meat-eaters too. Use frozen spinach if you're short of time.

INGREDIENTS

Serves 4
2 lb fresh spinach
1¼ cups vegetable or chicken broth
1 medium onion, finely chopped
1 garlic clove, crushed
¾ cup hazelnuts
2 tbsp chopped fresh basil
6 sheets lasagne
14oz can chopped tomatoes
1 cup low fat fromage frais
slivered hazlenuts and chopped parsley,
   to garnish

1 Preheat the oven to 400°F. Wash the spinach and place in a pan with just the water that clings to the leaves. Cook the spinach over a fairly high heat for 2 minutes until wilted. Drain well.

2 Heat 2 tbsp of the broth in a large pan and simmer the onion and garlic until soft. Stir in the spinach, hazelnuts, and basil.

3 In a large ovenproof dish, layer the spinach, lasagne, and tomatoes. Season well between the layers. Pour over the remaining broth. Spread the fromage frais over the top.

4 Bake the lasagne for about 45 minutes, or until golden brown. Serve hot, sprinkled with lines of slivered hazelnuts and chopped parsley.

COOK'S TIP
The flavor of hazelnuts is improved by roasting. Place them on a baking sheet and bake in a moderate oven, or under a hot broiler, until light golden.

NUTRITION NOTES	
Per portion:	
Energy	365Kcals/1532kJ
Fat	17g
Saturated fat	1.46g
Cholesterol	0.5mg
Fiber	8.16g

TAGLIATELLE WITH PEA AND BEAN SAUCE

A creamy pea sauce makes a wonderful combination with the crunchy young vegetables.

INGREDIENTS

Serves 4

1 tbsp olive oil
1 garlic clove, crushed
6 scallions, sliced
1 cup fresh or frozen baby peas, defrosted
12oz fresh young asparagus
2 tbsp chopped fresh sage, plus extra leaves, to garnish
finely grated rind of 2 lemons
1²/₃ cups vegetable broth or water
1½ cups fresh or frozen fava beans, defrosted
1lb tagliatelle
4 tbsp plain low fat yogurt

NUTRITION NOTES

Per portion:	
Energy	509 Kcals/2139kJ
Fat	6.75g
Saturated fat	0.95g
Cholesterol	0.6mg
Fiber	9.75g

1 Heat the oil in a pan. Add the garlic and scallions, and cook gently for about 2–3 minutes until softened.

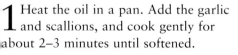

2 Add the peas and a third of the asparagus, together with the sage, lemon rind and broth or water. Simmer for about 10 minutes. Process in a food processor or blender until smooth.

3 Meanwhile remove the outer skins from the fava beans and discard.

4 Cut the remaining asparagus into 2in lengths, trimming off any tough fibrous stems, and blanch in boiling water for about 2 minutes.

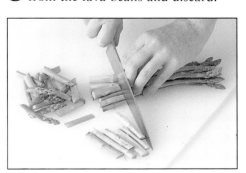

5 Cook the tagliatelle following the manufacturer's instructions until *al dente*. Drain well.

6 Add the cooked asparagus and shelled beans to the sauce, and reheat. Stir in the yogurt and toss into the tagliatelle. Garnish with a few extra sage leaves, and serve immediately.

COOK'S TIP
Frozen peas and beans have been suggested as an option here to cut down the preparation time, but the dish tastes even better if you use fresh young vegetables when in season.

PASTA WITH CHICK PEA SAUCE

INGREDIENTS

Serves 4
2 cups pasta
1 tsp olive oil
1 small onion, finely chopped
1 garlic clove, crushed
1 celery stalk, finely chopped
15oz can chick peas, drained
1 cup tomato sauce
salt and black pepper
chopped fresh parsley, to garnish

1 Heat the olive oil in a nonstick pan and sauté the onion, garlic, and celery until softened, not browned. Stir in the chick peas and tomato sauce, then cover and simmer for about 15 minutes.

2 Cook the pasta in a large pan of boiling, lightly salted water until just tender. Drain the pasta and toss into the sauce, then season to taste with salt and pepper. Sprinkle with chopped fresh parsley, then serve hot.

NUTRITION NOTES

Per portion:	
Energy	374Kcals/1570kJ
Fat	4.44g
Saturated fat	0.32g
Cholesterol	0
Fiber	6.41g

PEPERONATA PIZZA

INGREDIENTS

Makes 2 large pizzas
4 cups flour
pinch of salt
1 envelope active dry yeast
about 1½ cups warm water

For the topping
1 onion, sliced
2 tsp olive oil
2 large red and 2 yellow bell peppers,
  seeded and sliced
1 garlic clove, crushed
14oz can tomatoes
8 pitted ripe olives, halved
salt and black pepper

1 To make the dough, sift the flour and salt into a bowl and stir in the yeast. Stir in just enough warm water to mix to a soft dough.

2 Knead for 5 minutes until smooth. Cover and leave in a warm place for about 1 hour, or until doubled in size.

3 To make the topping, sauté the onion in the oil until soft, then stir in the peppers, garlic, and tomatoes. Cover and simmer for 30 minutes, until no liquid remains. Season to taste.

4 Preheat the oven to 450°F. Divide the dough in half and press out each piece on a lightly oiled baking sheet to a 11in round, turning up the edges slightly.

5 Spread over the topping, dot with olives, and bake for 15–20 minutes. Serve hot or cold, with salad.

NUTRITION NOTES

Per portion:	
Energy	965Kcals/4052kJ
Fat	9.04g
Saturated fat	1.07g
Cholesterol	0
Fiber	14.51g

Tabbouleh with Fennel

A fresh salad originating in the Middle East that is perfect for a summer lunch. Serve with lettuce and pita bread.

Ingredients

Serves 4

1¼ cups bulgur wheat
2 fennel bulbs
1 small red chili, seeded and chopped
1 celery stalk, finely sliced
2 tbsp olive oil
finely grated rind and juice of
　2 lemons
6–8 scallions, chopped
6 tbsp chopped fresh mint
6 tbsp chopped fresh parsley
1 pomegranate, seeded
salt and black pepper

Nutrition Notes

Per portion:

Energy	188Kcals/791kJ
Fat	4.67g
Saturated fat	0.62g
Cholesterol	0
Fiber	2.17g

1 Place the bulgur wheat in a bowl and pour over enough cold water to cover. Leave to stand for 30 minutes.

2 Drain the wheat through a strainer, pressing out any excess water using a spoon.

3 Halve the fennel bulbs and carefully cut them into very fine slices with a sharp knife.

4 Mix all the remaining ingredients together, including the soaked bulgur wheat and fennel. Season well, cover, and set aside for 30 minutes before serving.

Cook's Tip

Fennel has a very distinctive aniseed flavor. When you are buying fennel, choose well-rounded bulbs which are pale green to white in color. Avoid any that are deep green. Fennel never goes out of season – it is available all year round.

SWEET VEGETABLE COUSCOUS

A wonderful combination of sweet vegetables and spices, this makes a substantial winter dish.

INGREDIENTS

Serves 4–6

generous pinch of saffron threads
3 tbsp boiling water
1 tbsp olive oil
1 red onion, sliced
2 garlic cloves
1–2 red chilies, seeded and finely chopped
½ tsp ground ginger
½ tsp ground cinnamon
14oz can chopped tomatoes
1¼ cups fresh vegetable broth or water
4 carrots, peeled and cut into ¼in slices
2 turnips, peeled and cut into ¾in cubes
1lb sweet potatoes, peeled and cut into ¾in cubes
⅔ cup raisins
2 zucchini, cut into ¼in slices
14oz can chick-peas, drained and rinsed
3 tbsp chopped fresh parsley
3 tbsp chopped fresh cilantro
4 cups quick-cook couscous

1 Leave the saffron to infuse in the boiling water.

2 Heat the oil in a large saucepan or flameproof casserole. Add the onion, garlic and chilies, and cook gently for about 5 minutes.

3 Add the ginger and cinnamon to the pan or casserole, and cook gently for 1–2 minutes more.

4 Add the tomatoes, broth or water, saffron and liquid, carrots, turnips, sweet potatoes and raisins, cover and simmer for 25 minutes more.

5 Add the zucchini, chick-peas, parsley and cilantro, and cook for 10 minutes more.

6 Meanwhile prepare the couscous following the manufacturer's instructions, and then serve with the prepared vegetables.

NUTRITION NOTES

Per portion:

Energy	570Kcals/2393kJ
Fat	7.02g
Saturated fat	0.83g
Cholesterol	0
Fiber	10.04g

COOK'S TIP

Vegetable broth can be made from a variety of uncooked vegetables. These can include the outer leaves of cabbage, lettuce and other greens, carrot peelings, leeks as well as parsnips.

THAI FRAGRANT RICE

A lovely, soft, fluffy rice dish, perfumed with delicious and fresh lemon grass.

INGREDIENTS

Serves 4

1 piece lemon grass
2 limes
1⅓ cups brown basmati rice
1 tbsp olive oil
1 onion, chopped
1in piece fresh ginger root, peeled and finely chopped
1½ tsp cilantro seeds
1½ tsp cumin seeds
3⅔ cups vegetable broth
4 tbsp chopped fresh cilantro
lime wedges, to serve

COOK'S TIP
Other varieties of rice, such as white basmati or long grain, can be used for this dish but you will need to adjust the cooking times as necessary.

1 Finely chop the lemon grass and remove the zest from the limes.

2 Rinse the rice in cold water. Drain through a strainer.

3 Heat the oil in a large saucepan and add the onion and spices and cook gently for about 2–3 minutes.

4 Add the rice and cook for 1 minute more, then add the broth or water and bring to the boil. Reduce the heat to very low and cover the pan. Cook gently for about 30 minutes then check the rice. If it is still crunchy, cover the pan again with the lid and leave for 3–5 minutes more. Remove the pan from the heat.

5 Stir in the fresh cilantro, fluff up the grains, cover and keep warm for 10 minutes. Serve with lime wedges.

NUTRITION NOTES

Per portion:	
Energy	259Kcals/1087kJ
Fat	5.27g
Saturated fat	0.81g
Cholesterol	0
Fiber	1.49g

PUMPKIN AND PISTACHIO RISOTTO

This elegant combination of creamy golden rice and orange pumpkin can be made as pale or bright as you like – simply add different quantities of saffron.

INGREDIENTS

Serves 4

5 cups vegetable broth or water
generous pinch of saffron threads
2 tbsp olive oil
1 onion, chopped
2 garlic cloves, crushed
2lb pumpkin, peeled, seeded and cut
  into ¾in cubes
2 cups arborio rice
⅞ cup dry white wine
1 tbsp finely grated Parmesan cheese
½ cup pistachios
3 tbsp chopped fresh marjoram or
  oregano, plus a few extra leaves,
  to garnish
salt, freshly grated nutmeg and black
  pepper

NUTRITION NOTES

Per portion:

Energy	630Kcals/2646kJ
Fat	15.24g
Saturated fat	2.66g
Cholesterol	3.75mg
Fiber	2.59g

1 Bring the broth or water to a boil and reduce to a low simmer. Ladle a little liquid into a small bowl. Add the saffron threads and leave to infuse.

2 Heat the oil in a saucepan or flameproof casserole. Add the onion and garlic, and cook for 5 minutes until softened. Add the pumpkin and rice and cook for a few minutes more until the rice looks transparent.

3 Pour in the wine and allow it to boil hard. When it is absorbed add a quarter of the broth or water and the infused saffron and liquid. Stir until all the liquid is absorbed.

4 Gradually add a ladleful of broth or water at a time, allowing the rice to absorb the liquid before adding more and stir constantly.

5 Cook the rice for about 25–30 minutes or until *al dente*. Stir in the Parmesan cheese, cover the pan and leave to stand for 5 minutes.

6 To finish, stir in the pistachios and marjoram or oregano. Season to taste with a little salt, nutmeg and pepper, and sprinkle over a few extra marjoram or oregano leaves.

COOK'S TIP
Italian arborio rice is a special short grain rice that gives an authentic creamy consistency.

CORN KERNEL PANCAKES

These crisp pancakes are delicious to serve as a snack lunch, or as a light supper with a crisp mixed salad.

INGREDIENTS

Serves 4, makes about 12
1 cup self-rising flour
1 egg white
⅔ cup skim milk
7oz can corn kernels, drained
oil, for brushing
salt and black pepper
tomato chutney, to serve

1 Place the flour, egg white, and skim milk in a food processor or blender with half the corn and process until smooth.

2 Season the batter well and add the remaining corn.

3 Heat a frying pan and brush with oil. Drop in tablespoons of batter and cook until set. Turn over the pancakes and cook the other side until golden. Serve hot with tomato chutney.

NUTRITION NOTES

Per portion:

Energy	162Kcals/680kJ
Fat	0.89g
Saturated fat	0.14g
Cholesterol	0.75mg
Fiber	1.49g

BAKED POLENTA WITH TOMATOES

INGREDIENTS

Serves 4
3⅔ cups broth
scant 1¼ cups polenta (coarse corn-meal)
4 tbsp chopped fresh sage
1 tsp olive oil
2 beefsteak tomatoes, sliced
1 tbsp grated Parmesan cheese
salt and black pepper

1 Bring the broth to a boil in a large saucepan, then gradually stir in the polenta.

2 Continue stirring the polenta over moderate heat for about 5 minutes, until the mixture begins to come away from the sides of the pan. Stir in the chopped sage and season well, then spoon the polenta into a lightly oiled, shallow 9x13 in pan and spread evenly. Leave to cool.

3 Preheat the oven to 400°F. Cut the cooled polenta into 24 squares using a sharp knife.

4 Arrange the polenta overlapping with tomato slices in a lightly oiled, shallow ovenproof dish. Sprinkle with Parmesan and bake for 20 minutes, or until golden brown. Serve hot.

NUTRITION NOTES

Per portion:

Energy	200Kcals/842kJ
Fat	3.8g
Saturated fat	0.77g
Cholesterol	1.88mg
Fiber	1.71g

MEAT AND POULTRY

There's no reason why meat should not be a valuable part of a low-fat, low cholesterol diet, but you need to make careful choices when shopping and adapt preparation and cooking methods to keep fats to a minimum. Poultry is an obvious choice for a low-fat diet; endlessly versatile and economical, it is mostly very low in fat, and much of the fat it does contain is low in saturates. Tempt your family with dishes such as Sausage and Beans with Dumplings, Macaroni and Cheese with Turkey and Barbecued Chicken. You'll soon discover that meat and poultry have a full place to play in a low-fat, low cholesterol diet.

THAI BEEF SALAD

A hearty salad of beef, laced with a chili and lime dressing.

INGREDIENTS

Serves 6

6 lean sirloin steaks, 3oz each
1 red onion, finely sliced
$\frac{1}{2}$ cucumber, finely sliced
  into matchsticks
1 lemongrass stalk, finely chopped
2 tbsp chopped scallions
juice of 2 limes
1–2 tbsp fish sauce
2–4 red chilies, finely sliced, to garnish
cilantro, Chinese mustard cress and
  mint leaves, to garnish

NUTRITION NOTES

Per portion:

Energy	101Kcals/424kJ
Fat	3.8g
Saturated fat	1.7g
Cholesterol	33.4mg
Fiber	0.28g

COOK'S TIP

Round or tenderloin steaks would work just as well in this recipe. Choose good-quality lean steaks and remove and discard any visible fat.

1 Broil the sirloin steaks until they are medium-rare, then allow to rest for 10–15 minutes.

2 When cool, thinly slice the beef and put the slices in a large bowl.

3 Add the sliced onion, cucumber matchsticks and lemongrass.

4 Add the scallions. Toss and season with lime juice and fish sauce. Serve at room temperature or chilled, garnished with the chilies, cilantro, mustard cress and mint.

SPICED LAMB WITH VEGETABLE COUSCOUS

A delicious stew of lamb and vegetables served with couscous.

INGREDIENTS

Serves 6

12 ounces lean lamb cutlet, cut into ¾-inch cubes
2 tbsp whole-wheat flour, seasoned
2 tsp sunflower oil
1 onion, chopped
2 garlic cloves, crushed
1 red bell pepper, seeded and diced
1 tsp ground coriander
1 tsp ground cumin
1 tsp ground allspice
½ tsp chili powder
1 cup lamb or beef stock
14-ounce can chopped tomatoes
6 ounces carrots, sliced
6 ounces parsnips, sliced
6 ounces zucchini sliced
6 ounces small mushrooms, quartered
7 ounces fava beans
⅓ cup golden raisins
1 pound quick-cooking couscous
salt and ground black pepper
cilantro, to garnish

1 Toss the lamb in the flour. Heat the oil in a large saucepan and add the lamb, onion, garlic and pepper. Cook for 5 minutes, stirring frequently.

NUTRITION NOTES

Per portion:
Energy	439Kcals/1844kJ
Fat	8.6g
Saturated fat	2.88g
Cholesterol	49.6mg
Fiber	7.2g

2 Add any remaining flour and the spices and cook for 1 minute, stirring.

3 Gradually add the stock, stirring continuously, then add the tomatoes, carrots and parsnips and mix well. Bring to the boil, stirring then cover and simmer for 30 minutes, stirring occasionally.

4 Add the zucchini, mushrooms, fava beans and golden raisins. Cover, return to a boil and simmer for another 20–30 minutes, stirring occasionally, until the lamb and vegetables are tender. Season to taste.

5 Meanwhile, soak the couscous and steam in a lined colander over a pan of boiling water for about 20 minutes, until cooked, or according to the package instructions. Pile the cooked couscous onto a warmed serving platter or individual plates and top with the lamb and vegetable stew. Garnish with cilantro and serve immediately.

BEEF AND LENTIL PIES

In this variation of shepherd's pie, lentils are substituted for some of the meat to lower the fat content and increase the fiber. Some red meat is included to boost the iron content.

INGREDIENTS

Serves 4
1 cup green lentils
8 ounces extra-lean ground beef
1 onion, chopped
2 celery sticks, chopped
1 large carrot, chopped
1 garlic clove, crushed
15-ounce can chopped tomatoes
2 tsp brewer's yeast powder
1 bay leaf

For the topping
1 lb potatoes, peeled and cut into large
  chunks
1 lb parsnips, peeled and cut into large
  chunks
4 tbsp low-fat plain yogurt
3 tbsp chopped chives
4 tsp freshly grated Parmesan
  cheese
2 tomatoes, sliced
¼ cup pine nuts (optional)

1 Place the lentils in a pan and pour in cold water to cover. Bring to a boil, then boil for 10 minutes.

2 Meanwhile, brown the beef in a saucepan, without any extra fat. Stir in the onion, celery, carrot and garlic. Cook gently for 5 minutes, then stir in the tomatoes.

3 Drain the lentils, reserving 1¼ cups of the cooking water in a measuring cup. Add the lentils to the meat mixture, then dissolve the yeast powder in the cooking water and stir it in. Add the bay leaf and bring to a boil, then lower the heat, cover the pan and cook gently for 20 minutes.

NUTRITION NOTES	
Per portion:	
Energy	470Kcals/1985kJ
Fat	10.6g
Saturated fat	2.17g
Cholesterol	36.3mg
Fiber	13.3g

4 Make the topping. Bring a saucepan of lighly salted water to a boil and cook the potatoes and parsnips for about 15 minutes, until tender. Drain, turn into a bowl, and mash with the yogurt and chives. Preheat the broiler.

5 Remove the bay leaf and divide the mixture among four small dishes. Spoon over the potato mixture. Sprinkle with Parmesan and garnish with tomato slices. Sprinkle pine nuts over the top, if using, and broil the pies for a few minutes until the topping is crisp and golden.

SAUSAGE AND BEANS WITH DUMPLINGS

Sausages needn't be totally banned on a low fat diet, but choose them carefully. If you are unable to find a reduced-fat variety, choose turkey sausages instead, and always drain off any fat during cooking.

INGREDIENTS

Serves 4

1 lb half-fat sausages
1 medium onion, thinly sliced
1 green bell pepper, seeded and diced
1 small red chili, sliced, or ½ tsp chili sauce
14oz can chopped tomatoes
1 cup beef broth
15oz can red kidney beans, drained
salt and black pepper

For the dumplings
2½ cups flour
2 tsp baking powder
1 cup cottage cheese

1 Cook the sausages without fat in a nonstick pan until brown. Add the onion and pepper. Stir in the chili, tomatoes, and broth; bring to a boil.

NUTRITION NOTES

Per portion:	
Energy	574Kcals/2409kJ
Fat	13.09g
Saturated fat	0.15g
Cholesterol	52.31mg
Fiber	9.59g

2 Cover and simmer gently for 15–20 minutes, then add the beans and bring to a boil.

3 To make the dumplings, sift the flour and baking powder together and add enough water to mix to a firm dough. Roll out thinly and stamp out 16–18 rounds using a 3in cutter.

4 Place a small spoonful of cottage cheese on each round and bring the edges of the dough together, pinching to enclose. Arrange the dumplings over the sausages in the pan, cover the pan, and simmer for 10–12 minutes, until the dumplings are puffed. Serve hot.

HONEY-ROAST PORK WITH HERBS

Herbs and honey add flavor and sweetness to tenderloin—the leanest cut of pork.

INGREDIENTS

Serves 4

1 lb pork tenderloin
2 tbsp thick honey
2 tbsp Dijon mustard
1 tsp chopped fresh rosemary
½ tsp chopped fresh thyme
¼ tsp pink and green peppercorns
fresh rosemary and thyme sprigs,
*   to garnish*
potato gratin and cauliflower, to serve

For the red onion confit

4 red onions
1½ cups vegetable stock
1 tbsp red wine vinegar
1 tbsp superfine sugar
1 garlic clove, crushed
2 tbsp ruby port
pinch of salt

1 Pre-heat the oven to 350°F. Trim off any visible fat from the pork. Put the honey, mustard, rosemary and thyme in a small bowl and mix them together well.

2 Crush the peppercorns using a pestle and mortar. Spread the honey mixture over the pork and sprinkle with the crushed peppercorns. Place in a nonstick roasting pan and cook in the preheated oven for 35–45 minutes.

3 For the red onion confit, slice the onions into rings and put them into a heavy saucepan.

4 Add the stock, vinegar, sugar and garlic clove to the saucepan. Bring to a boil, then reduce the heat. Cover and simmer for 15 minutes.

5 Uncover and pour in the port and continue to simmer, stirring occasionally, until the onions are soft and the juices thick and syrupy. Season to taste with salt.

6 Cut the pork into slices and arrange on four warmed plates. Serve garnished with rosemary and thyme and accompanied with the red onion confit, potato gratin and cauliflower.

NUTRITION NOTES

Per portion:

Energy	258Kcals/1080kJ
Fat	8.9g
Saturated fat	2.92g
Cholesterol	77.6mg
Fiber	1.2g

MACARONI AND CHEESE WITH TURKEY

A tasty low fat alternative to macaroni and cheese, the addition of smoked turkey bacon makes this dish a family favorite. Serve with warm Italian bread and a mixed green salad.

NUTRITION NOTES

Per portion:	
Energy	152Kcals/637kJ
Fat	2.8g
Saturated fat	0.7g
Cholesterol	12mg
Fiber	1.1g

INGREDIENTS

Serves 4

1 medium onion, chopped
⅔ cup vegetable or chicken stock
2 tbsp low fat margarine
3 tbsp all-purpose flour
¼ cup skim milk
2oz reduced fat Cheddar
  cheese, grated
1 tsp dry mustard
8oz macaroni
4 turkey bacon strips, cut in half
2–3 firm tomatoes, sliced
a few fresh basil leaves
1 tbsp grated Parmesan cheese
salt and black pepper

1 Put the chopped onion and stock into a nonstick frying pan. Bring to a boil, stirring occasionally, and cook for 5–6 minutes or until the stock has reduced entirely and the onion is transparent.

2 Put the margarine, flour, milk and seasoning into a saucepan and whisk together over the heat until thickened and smooth. Set aside and add the cheese, mustard and onion.

3 Cook the macaroni in a large pot of boiling, salted water according to the instructions on the package. Preheat the broiler. Drain the macaroni thoroughly and stir into the sauce. Transfer to a shallow ovenproof dish.

4 Arrange the turkey bacon and tomatoes overlapping on top of the macaroni and cheese. Tuck in the basil leaves, then sprinkle with Parmesan and broil to lightly brown the top.

THAI CHICKEN AND VEGETABLE STIR-FRY

Serves 4

*1 piece lemongrass (or the rind of
½ lemon)*
½in piece fresh ginger
1 large garlic clove
2 tbsp sunflower oil
10oz lean chicken
½ red bell pepper, seeded and sliced
½ green bell pepper, seeded and sliced
4 scallions, chopped
2 medium carrots, cut into matchsticks
4oz thin green beans
1oz peanuts, lightly crushed
2 tbsp oyster sauce
pinch of sugar
salt and black pepper
cilantro leaves, to garnish
steamed rice, to serve

NUTRITION NOTES

Per portion:
Energy	203Kcals/849kJ
Fat	11.0g
Saturated fat	2.0g
Cholesterol	29.6mg
Fiber	2.6g

1 Thinly slice the lemongrass or lemon rind. Peel and chop the ginger and garlic. Heat the oil in a frying pan over high heat. Add the lemongrass or lemon rind, ginger and garlic, and stir-fry for 30 seconds, until brown.

2 Add the chicken and stir-fry for 2 minutes. Then add all the vegetables and stir-fry for 4–5 minutes, until the chicken is cooked and the vegetables are almost cooked.

3 Finally, stir in the peanuts, oyster sauce, sugar and seasoning to taste. Stir-fry for another minute to blend the flavors. Serve immediately, sprinkled with the cilantro leaves and accompanied by steamed rice.

COOK'S TIP
Make this quick supper dish a little hotter by adding more fresh ginger, if desired.

BARBECUED CHICKEN

INGREDIENTS

Serves 4 or 8

8 small chicken pieces
2 limes, cut into wedges, 2 red chilies,
  finely sliced, and 2 lemongrass stalks,
  to garnish
rice, to serve

For the marinade

2 lemongrass stalks, chopped
1in piece fresh ginger
6 garlic cloves
4 shallots
$^1/_2$ bunch cilantro
1 tbsp sugar
$^1/_2$ cup coconut milk
2 tbsp fish sauce
2 tbsp soy sauce

COOK'S TIP
Don't eat the skin of the chicken –
it's only left on to keep the flesh
moist during cooking. Coconut
milk makes a good base for a
marinade or sauce, as it is low in
calories and fat.

NUTRITION NOTES

Per portion (for 8):

Energy	100Kcals/420kJ
Fat	2.8g
Saturated fat	0.89g
Cholesterol	35.6mg
Fiber	0.3g

1 To make the marinade, put all the ingredients into a food processor and process until smooth.

2 Put the chicken pieces in a dish and add the marinade. Set aside in a cool place to marinate for at least 4 hours or overnight.

3 Preheat the oven to 400°F. Put the chicken pieces on a rack on a baking tray. Brush the chicken with the marinade and bake for 20–30 minutes, or until the chicken is cooked and golden brown. Turn the pieces over halfway through cooking and brush with more marinade.

4 Garnish with lime wedges, finely sliced red chilies and lemongrass stalks. Serve with rice.

HOT CHICKEN CURRY

This curry has a flavorful thick sauce, and includes red and green bell peppers for extra color. Serve with whole-wheat chapatis or plain boiled rice.

INGREDIENTS

Serves 4

2 tbsp corn oil
¼ tsp fenugreek seeds
¼ tsp onion seeds
2 onions, chopped
1 garlic clove, crushed
½ tsp grated fresh ginger root
1 tsp ground cilantro
1 tsp chili powder
1 tsp salt
14oz can tomatoes
2 tbsp lemon juice
12oz chicken without skin and
   bone, cubed
2 tbsp chopped fresh cilantro
3 green chilies, chopped
½ red bell pepper, cut into chunks
½ green bell pepper, cut into chunks
fresh cilantro leaves, to garnish

2 Meanwhile, in a separate bowl, mix together the ground cilantro, chili powder, salt, tomatoes and lemon juice.

4 Add the chicken and stir-fry for about 5–7 minutes. Take care not to overcook the chicken.

1 Heat the oil in a medium saucepan, and fry the fenugreek and onion seeds until they turn a shade darker. Add the onions, garlic and ginger and fry for about 5 minutes until the onions are golden. Lower the heat to very low.

3 Pour this mixture into the pan and turn up the heat to medium. Stir-fry for about 3 minutes.

5 Add the fresh cilantro, green chilies and the sliced bell peppers. Lower the heat, cover, and simmer for about 10 minutes until cooked. Serve hot, garnished with fresh cilantro leaves.

COOK'S TIP
For a milder version of this delicious curry, simply omit some or all of the fresh green chilies.

NUTRITION NOTES	
Per portion:	
Energy	216Kcals/900kJ
Fat	10.0g
Saturated fat	2.06g
Cholesterol	49.9mg
Fiber	2.2g

FISH AND SEAFOOD

Fish is ideally designed for healthy, quick meals. Most types of fish are very low in fat and high in protein, and even oily fish is high in essential fatty acids that boost 'good' HDL cholesterol. Furthermore, some fish, such as shrimp, though high in cholesterol, are low in fats, and it is now believed that it is the amount of saturated fat in the diet that most affects blood cholesterol levels. Healthy, and easy to cook, fish is perfect for absorbing the exotic flavors of different herbs, spices and marinades—try Glazed Garlic Shrimp with its refreshing tangy lemon and mango chutney sauce for a delicious, healthy meal.

HADDOCK AND BROCCOLI CHOWDER

A warming main-meal soup for hearty appetites.

INGREDIENTS

Serves 4
4 scallions, sliced
1 lb new potatoes, diced
1¼ cups fish broth or water
1¼ cups skim milk
1 bay leaf
2 cups broccoli florets, sliced
1 lb smoked haddock fillets, skinned
7oz can corn kernels, drained
black pepper
chopped scallions, to garnish

1 Place the scallions and potatoes in a large saucepan and add the broth, milk, and bay leaf. Bring the soup to a boil, then cover the pan and simmer for 10 minutes.

2 Add the broccoli to the pan. Cut the fish into bite-sized chunks and add to the pan with the corn kernels.

3 Season the soup well with black pepper, then cover the pan and simmer for 5 minutes more, or until the fish is cooked through. Remove the bay leaf and scatter over the scallions. Serve hot, with crusty bread.

COOK'S TIP
When new potatoes are not available, old ones can be used, but choose a waxy variety that will not disintegrate.

NUTRITION NOTES

Per portion:
Energy	268Kcals/1124kJ
Fat	2.19g
Saturated fat	0.27g
Cholesterol	57.75mg
Fiber	3.36g

TUNA AND CORN FISH CAKES

These economical little tuna fish cakes are quick to make. Either use fresh mashed potatoes, or make a less fussy version with instant mashed potatoes.

INGREDIENTS

Serves 4

1¼ cups cooked mashed
    potatoes
7oz can tuna in vegetable oil,
    drained
¾ cup canned or frozen corn
    kernels
2 tbsp chopped fresh parsley
1 cup fresh white or whole-wheat
    bread crumbs
salt and black pepper
lemon wedges, to serve

1 Place the mashed potato in a bowl and stir in the tuna, corn kernels, and chopped parsley.

2 Season to taste with salt and pepper, then shape into eight patty shapes with your hands.

3 Spread out the bread crumbs on a plate and press the fish cakes into the bread crumbs to coat lightly, then place on a baking sheet.

4 Cook the fish cakes under a moderately hot broiler until crisp and golden brown, turning once. Serve hot, with lemon wedges and fresh vegetables.

COOK'S TIP
For simple variations that are just as pleasing and nutritious, try using canned sardines, red or pink salmon, or smoked mackerel in place of the tuna.

NUTRITION NOTES

Per portion:	
Energy	203Kcals/852kJ
Fat	4.62g
Saturated fat	0.81g
Cholesterol	21.25mg
Fiber	1.82g

Fish Fillets with a Chili Sauce

Fish fillets, marinated with fresh cilantro and lemon juice, then broiled and served with a chili sauce, are delicious accompanied with saffron rice.

Ingredients

Serves 4

4 flatfish fillets, such as plaice, sole or flounder, about 4oz each
2 tbsp lemon juice
1 tbsp finely chopped fresh cilantro
1 tbsp vegetable oil
lime wedges and cilantro leaves, to garnish

For the sauce

1 tsp grated fresh ginger root
2 tbsp tomato paste
1 tsp sugar
1 tsp salt
1 tbsp chili sauce
1 tbsp malt vinegar
1¼ cups water

1 Rinse, pat dry and place the fish fillets in a medium bowl. Add the lemon juice, fresh cilantro and oil and rub into the fish. Leave to marinate for at least 1 hour. The flavor will improve if you can leave it for longer.

2 To make the sauce, mix together all the sauce ingredients, pour into a small saucepan and simmer over a low heat for about 6 minutes, stirring occasionally.

3 Preheat the broiler to medium. Cook the fillets under the broiler for about 5–7 minutes.

4 When the fillets are cooked, remove and arrange them on a warmed serving dish.

5 The chili sauce should now be fairly thick – about the consistency of a thick chicken soup.

6 Spoon the sauce over the fillets, garnish with the lime wedges and cilantro leaves, and serve with rice.

Nutrition Notes	
Per portion:	
Energy	142Kcals/599kJ
Fat	5.3g
Saturated fat	0.75g
Cholesterol	48.3mg
Fiber	0.2g

GLAZED GARLIC SHRIMP

A fairly simple and quick dish to prepare, it is best to peel the shrimp as this helps them to absorb maximum flavor. Serve as a main course with a variety of accompaniments, or with a salad as an appetizer.

INGREDIENTS

Serves 4

1 tbsp sunflower oil
3 garlic cloves, roughly chopped
3 tomatoes, chopped
½ tsp salt
1 tsp crushed dried red chilies
1 tsp lemon juice
1 tbsp mango chutney
1 green chili, chopped
15–20 cooked jumbo shrimp, peeled
fresh cilantro leaves and 2 chopped
    scallions, to garnish

NUTRITION NOTES

Per portion:	
Energy	101Kcals/421kJ
Fat	3.6g
Saturated fat	0.41g
Cholesterol	95.0mg
Fiber	0.9g

1 Heat the oil in a medium saucepan, and add the chopped garlic.

2 Lower the heat. Add the chopped tomatoes along with the salt, crushed chilies, lemon juice, mango chutney and chopped fresh chili.

3 Finally add the shrimp, turn up the heat and stir-fry quickly until they are heated through.

4 Transfer to a serving dish. Serve immediately garnished with fresh cilantro leaves and chopped scallions.

COD CREOLE

INGREDIENTS

Serves 4

1 lb cod fillets, skinned
1 tbsp lime or lemon juice
2 tsp olive oil
1 medium onion, finely chopped
1 green bell pepper, seeded and sliced
½ tsp cayenne pepper
½ tsp garlic salt
14oz can chopped tomatoes

NUTRITION NOTES

Per portion:
Energy	130Kcals/546kJ
Fat	2.61g
Saturated fat	0.38g
Cholesterol	51.75mg
Fiber	1.61g

1 Cut the cod fillets into bite-sized chunks and sprinkle with the lime or lemon juice.

2 In a large, nonstick pan, heat the olive oil and sauté the onion and pepper gently until softened. Add the cayenne pepper and garlic salt.

3 Stir in the cod with the chopped tomatoes. Bring to a boil, then cover and simmer for about 5 minutes, or until the fish flakes easily. Serve with boiled rice or potatoes.

FIVE-SPICE FISH

Chinese mixtures of spicy, sweet, and sour flavors are particularly successful with fish, and dinner is ready in minutes.

INGREDIENTS

Serves 4

4 white fish fillets, such as cod, haddock or flounder (about 6oz each)
1 tsp Chinese five-spice powder
4 tsp cornstarch
1 tbsp sesame or sunflower oil
3 scallions, shredded
1 tsp finely chopped ginger
5oz button mushrooms, sliced
4oz baby corn, sliced
2 tbsp soy sauce
3 tbsp dry sherry or apple juice
1 tsp sugar
salt and black pepper

1 Toss the fish in the five-spice powder and cornstarch to coat.

2 Heat the oil in a frying pan or wok and stir-fry the scallions, ginger, mushrooms, and corn for about 1 minute. Add the fish and cook for 2–3 minutes, turning once.

3 Mix together the soy sauce, sherry, and sugar, then pour over the fish. Simmer for 2 minutes, adjust the seasoning, then serve with noodles and stir-fried vegetables.

NUTRITION NOTES

Per portion:
Energy	213Kcals/893kJ
Fat	4.41g
Saturated fat	0.67g
Cholesterol	80.5mg
Fiber	1.08g

SHRIMP WITH VEGETABLES

This is a light and nutritious dish. It is excellent served either on a bed of lettuce leaves, with plain boiled rice or whole-wheat chapatis for a healthy meal.

INGREDIENTS

Serves 4

2 tbsp chopped fresh cilantro
1 tsp salt
2 green chilies, seeded if required
3 tbsp lemon juice
2 tbsp vegetable oil
20 cooked jumbo shrimp, peeled
1 zucchini, thickly sliced
1 onion, cut into 8 chunks
8 cherry tomatoes
8 baby corn
mixed salad leaves, to serve

NUTRITION NOTES

Per portion:

Energy	142Kcals/592kJ
Fat	6.6g
Saturated fat	0.68g
Cholesterol	125.4mg
Fiber	1.2g

1 Place the chopped cilantro, salt, green chilies, lemon juice and oil in a food processor or blender and process for a few seconds.

2 Remove the chili paste from the food processor or blender and transfer to a mixing bowl.

3 Add the peeled shrimp to the paste and stir to make sure that all the shrimp are well coated. Set aside to marinate for about 30 minutes.

4 Preheat the broiler to very hot, then turn the heat down to medium.

5 Arrange the vegetables and shrimp alternately on four skewers. When all the skewers are ready, place them under the preheated broiler for 5–7 minutes until cooked and browned.

6 Serve immediately on a bed of mixed salad leaves.

COOK'S TIP
Jumbo shrimp are a luxury, but worth choosing for a very special dinner party. For a more economical variation, substitute the jumbo shrimp with 2½ cups ordinary shrimp.

TUNA AND FLAGEOLET BEAN SALAD

Two cans of tuna fish form the basis of this delicious and easy-to-make storecupboard salad.

INGREDIENTS

Serves 4

6 tbsp reduced calorie mayonnaise
1 tsp mustard
2 tbsp capers
3 tbsp chopped fresh parsley
pinch of celery salt
2 x 7oz cans tuna in brine, drained
3 Bibb lettuces
14oz can flageolet beans, drained
12 cherry tomatoes, halved
14oz can baby artichoke hearts, halved
toasted sesame bread or sticks, to serve

NUTRITION NOTES

Per portion:

Energy	299Kcals/1255kJ
Fat	13.91g
Saturated fat	2.12g
Cholesterol	33mg
Fiber	6.36g

1 Combine the mayonnaise, mustard, capers and parsley in a mixing bowl. Season to taste with celery salt.

2 Flake the tuna into the dressing and toss gently.

3 Arrange the lettuce leaves on four plates, then spoon the tuna mixture on to the leaves.

COOK'S TIP
If flageolet beans are not available, use cannellini beans.

4 Spoon the flageolet beans to one side, followed by the tomatoes and artichoke hearts.

5 Serve with slices of toasted sesame bread or sticks.

VEGETABLES AND SALADS

We're very lucky to have a huge variety of fresh vegetables available all year round these days, so there is no excuse for not making maximum use of them at every opportunity, whether they form the basis of the main course, or are served as an accompaniment to meat or fish dishes. Be adventurous with vegetables: use them in different combinations or with exotic herbs and spices for new textures and flavors. Middle-Eastern Vegetable Stew with cumin and fresh mint is just one example. Take a fresh look at salads, too, and discover that they needn't be soaked in heavy, oily dressings to be tasty. Try tangy, yogurt dressings, cider vinegar and fromage frais.

SPICY BAKED POTATOES

INGREDIENTS

Serves 2–4

2 large baking potatoes
1 tsp sunflower oil
1 small onion, finely chopped
1in piece fresh ginger root, grated
1 tsp ground cumin
1 tsp ground coriander
½ tsp ground turmeric
garlic salt
plain yogurt and fresh cilantro sprigs,
* to serve*

1 Preheat the oven to 375°F. Prick the potatoes with a fork. Bake for 40 minutes, or until soft.

2 Cut the potatoes in half and scoop out the flesh. Heat the oil in a nonstick pan and sauté the onion for a few minutes to soften. Stir in the ginger, cumin, coriander, and turmeric.

3 Stir over low heat for about 2 minutes, then add the potato flesh, and garlic salt, to taste.

4 Cook the potato mixture for 2 minutes more, stirring occasionally. Spoon the mixture back into the potato shells and top each with a spoonful of plain yogurt and a sprig or two of fresh cilantro. Serve hot.

NUTRITION NOTES

Per portion:	
Energy	212Kcals/890kJ
Fat	2.54g
Saturated fat	0.31g
Cholesterol	0.4mg
Fiber	3.35g

TWO BEANS PROVENÇAL

INGREDIENTS

Serves 4

1 tsp olive oil
1 small onion, finely chopped
1 garlic clove, crushed
8oz haricot verts beans
8oz green beans
2 tomatoes, peeled and chopped
salt and black pepper

NUTRITION NOTES

Per portion:	
Energy	68Kcals/286kJ
Fat	1.76g
Saturated fat	0.13g
Cholesterol	0
Fibre	5.39g

1 Heat the oil in a heavy-based, or nonstick, pan and sauté the chopped onion over medium heat until softened but not browned.

2 Add the garlic, both the beans, and the tomatoes, then season well and cover tightly.

3 Cook over fairly low heat, shaking the pan occasionally, for about 30 minutes, or until the beans are tender. Serve hot.

SWEET POTATO AND CARROT SALAD

INGREDIENTS

Serves 4

1 sweet potato, peeled and
  roughly diced
2 carrots, cut into thick
  diagonal slices
3 tomatoes
8–10 iceberg lettuce leaves
¾ cup canned chick-peas, drained

For the dressing

1 tbsp clear honey
6 tbsp plain low fat yogurt
½ tsp salt
1 tsp coarsely ground black pepper

For the garnish

1 tbsp walnuts
1 tbsp golden raisins
1 small onion, cut into rings

NUTRITION NOTES

Per portion:	
Energy	147Kcals/614kJ
Fat	3.8g
Saturated fat	0.52g
Cholesterol	1.2mg
Fiber	3.4g

1 Place the potatoes in a large saucepan and cover with water. Bring to a boil and cook until soft but not mushy, cover the pan and set aside. Boil the carrots for a few minutes making sure they remain crunchy. Add to the sweet potatoes.

3 Slice the tops off the tomatoes, then scoop out and discard the seeds. Roughly chop the flesh.

5 For the dressing, blend together all the ingredients and beat together with a fork.

2 Drain the water from the sweet potatoes and carrots, and place together in a bowl.

4 Line a glass bowl with the lettuce leaves. Mix together the sweet potatoes, carrots, chick-peas and tomatoes, and place in the bowl.

6 Spoon the dressing over the salad o serve it in a separate bowl. Garnish the salad with the walnuts, golden raisins and onion rings.

LEMONY VEGETABLE PARCELS

INGREDIENTS

Serves 4

2 medium carrots
1 small rutabaga
1 large parsnip
1 leek, sliced
finely grated rind of ½ lemon
1 tbsp lemon juice
1 tbsp whole-grain mustard
1 tsp walnut or sunflower oil
salt and black pepper

1 Preheat the oven to 375°F. Peel the root vegetables and cut into ½ in cubes. Place in a large bowl, then add the sliced leek.

2 Stir the lemon rind and juice and the mustard into the vegetables and mix well, then season to taste.

3 Cut four 12 in squares of nonstick baking paper and brush them lightly with the oil.

4 Divide the vegetables among them. Roll up the paper from one side, then twist the ends firmly to seal.

5 Place the parcels on a baking sheet and bake for 50–55 minutes, or until the vegetables are just tender. Serve hot, with roast or broiled meats.

NUTRITION NOTES	
Per portion	
Energy	78Kcals/326kJ
Fat	2.06g
Saturated fat	0.08g
Cholesterol	0
Fiber	5.15g

MIDDLE-EASTERN VEGETABLE STEW

A spiced dish of mixed vegetables that can be served as a side dish or as a vegetarian main course. Children may prefer less chili.

INGREDIENTS

Serves 4–6

3 tbsp vegetable or chicken broth
1 green bell pepper, seeded and sliced
2 medium zucchini, sliced
2 medium carrots, sliced
2 celery sticks, sliced
2 medium potatoes, diced
14oz can chopped tomatoes
1 tsp chili powder
2 tbsp chopped fresh mint
1 tbsp ground cumin
14oz can chick peas, drained
salt and black pepper
mint sprigs, to garnish

1 Heat the vegetable or chicken broth in a large flameproof casserole until boiling, then add the sliced bell pepper, zucchini, carrot, and celery. Stir over high heat for 2–3 minutes, until the vegetables are just beginning to soften.

2 Add the potatoes, tomatoes, chili powder, mint, and cumin. Add the chick peas and bring to a boil.

3 Reduce the heat, cover the casserole, and simmer for 30 minutes, or until all the vegetables are tender. Season to taste with salt and pepper and serve hot, garnished with mint leaves.

COOK'S TIP
Chick peas are traditional in this type of Middle-Eastern dish, but if you prefer, red kidney beans or navy beans can be used instead.

NUTRITION NOTES

Per portion:

Energy	168Kcals/703kJ
Fat	3.16g
Saturated fat	0.12g
Cholesterol	0
Fiber	6.13g

SUMMER VEGETABLE BRAISE

Tender, young vegetables are ideal for quick cooking in a minimum of liquid. Use any mixture of the family's favorite vegetables, as long as they are of similar size.

INGREDIENTS

Serves 4

2½ cups baby carrots
2 cups sugar-snap peas or snow peas
1¼ cups baby corn
6 tbsp vegetable broth
2 tsp lime juice
salt and black pepper
chopped fresh parsley and snipped fresh
    chives, to garnish

1 Place the carrots, peas, and baby corn in a large heavy-based saucepan with the vegetable broth and lime juice. Bring to a boil.

2 Cover the pan and reduce the heat, then simmer for 6–8 minutes, shaking the pan occasionally, until the vegetables are just tender.

3 Season the vegetables to taste with salt and pepper, then stir in the chopped fresh parsley and snipped chives. Cook the vegetables for a few seconds more, stirring them once or twice until the herbs are well mixed, then serve at once, with broiled lamb chops or roast chicken.

COOK'S TIP
You can make this dish in the winter too, but cut larger, tougher vegetables into chunks and cook for slightly longer.

NUTRITION NOTES

Per portion:
Energy	36Kcals/152kJ
Fat	0.45g
Saturated fat	0
Cholesterol	0
Fiber	2.35g

ROSEMARY ROASTIES

These unusual roast potatoes use far less fat than traditional roast potatoes, and because they still have their skins they not only absorb less oil but have more flavor too.

INGREDIENTS

Serves 4
2 lb small red potatoes
2 tsp walnut or sunflower oil
2 tbsp fresh rosemary leaves
salt and paprika

1 Preheat the oven to 475°F. Leave the potatoes whole with the peel on, or if large, cut in half. Place the potatoes in a large pan of cold water and bring to a boil. Drain well.

2 Drizzle the walnut or sunflower oil over the potatoes and shake the pan to coat them evenly.

3 Tip the potatoes into a shallow roasting pan. Sprinkle with rosemary, salt, and paprika. Roast for 30 minutes or until crisp. Serve hot.

NUTRITION NOTES

Per portion:
Energy	205Kcals/865kJ
Fat	2.22g
Saturated fat	0.19g
Cholesterol	0
Fiber	3.25g

BAKED ZUCCHINI IN TOMATO SAUCE

INGREDIENTS

Serves 4
1 tsp olive oil
3 large zucchini, thinly sliced
½ small red onion, finely chopped
1¼ cups tomato sauce
2 tbsp chopped fresh thyme
garlic salt and black pepper
fresh thyme sprigs, to garnish

1 Preheat the oven to 375°F. Brush an ovenproof dish with olive oil. Arrange half the zucchini and onion in the dish.

2 Spoon half the tomato sauce over the vegetables and sprinkle with some of the fresh thyme, then season to taste with garlic salt and pepper.

3 Arrange the remaining zucchini and onion in the dish on top of the sauce, then season to taste with more garlic salt and pepper. Spoon over the remaining sauce and spread evenly.

4 Cover the dish with foil, then bake for 40–45 minutes, or until the zucchini is tender. Garnish with sprigs of thyme and serve hot.

NUTRITION NOTES

Per portion:
Energy	49Kcals/205kJ
Fat	1.43g
Saturated fat	0.22g
Cholesterol	0
Fiber	1.73g

RED CABBAGE IN PORT AND RED WINE

A sweet and sour, spicy red cabbage dish, with the added crunch of walnuts.

NUTRITION NOTES

Per portion:

Energy	336Kcals/1409kJ
Fat	15.41g
Saturated fat	1.58g
Cholesterol	0
Fiber	4.31g

INGREDIENTS

Serves 6
1 tbsp walnut oil
1 onion, sliced
2 whole star anise
1 tsp ground cinnamon
pinch of ground cloves
5 cups finely shredded red cabbage
2 tbsp dark brown sugar
3 tbsp red wine vinegar
1¼ cups red wine
⅔ cup port
2 pears, cut into ½in cubes
⅔ cup raisins
½ cup walnut halves
salt and black pepper

1 Heat the oil in a large flameproof casserole. Add the onion and cook gently for about 5 minutes until softened.

2 Add the star anise, cinnamon, cloves and cabbage, and cook for 3 minutes more.

3 Stir in the sugar, vinegar, red wine and port. Cover the pan and simmer gently for 10 minutes, stirring occasionally.

4 Stir in the cubed pears and raisins, and cook for 10 minutes more or until the cabbage is tender. Season to taste. Mix in the walnut halves and serve immediately.

COOK'S TIP
If you are unable to buy pre-packaged walnut halves, buy whole ones and shell them.

WATERCRESS AND POTATO SALAD

New potatoes are equally good hot or cold, and this colorful, nutritious salad is an ideal way of making the most of them.

INGREDIENTS

Serves 4

1 lb small new potatoes, unpeeled
1 bunch watercress
1½ cups cherry tomatoes, halved
2 tbsp pumpkin seeds
3 tbsp low fat fromage frais
1 tbsp cider vinegar
1 tsp brown sugar
salt and paprika

1 Cook the potatoes in lightly salted, boiling water until just tender, then drain and leave to cool.

2 Toss together the potatoes, watercress, tomatoes, and pumpkin seeds.

3 Place the fromage frais, vinegar, sugar, salt, and paprika in a screwtop jar and shake well to mix. Pour over the salad just before serving.

NUTRITION NOTES

Per portion:

Energy	150Kcals/630kJ
Fat	4.15g
Saturated fat	0.81g
Cholesterol	0.11mg
Fiber	2.55g

COOK'S TIP
If you are packing this salad for a picnic, take the dressing in the jar and toss in just before serving.

DESSERTS, CAKES AND BAKES

Dessert lovers will be glad to learn that desserts need not be taboo in low-fat and low cholesterol diets. There are lots of ways to cook delicious desserts, cakes and bakes without the need for rich, high-fat mixtures. The rapidly expanding range of low-fat dairy products such as fromage frais, yogurt and creme fraîche means that lighter, far less rich desserts—without sacrificing enjoyment—are now possible. Classic dishes can be made a little less sinful by addng less fat and more flavor through the addition of nuts, fruits and spices—try Sunflower-Raisin Scones and Apricot and Orange Roulade.

GOLDEN GINGER COMPOTE

Warm, spicy and full of sun-ripened ingredients – this is the perfect winter dessert.

INGREDIENTS

Serves 4
2 cups kumquats
1¼ cups dried apricots
2 tbsp golden raisins
1⅔ cups water
1 orange
1in piece fresh ginger root
4 cardamom pods
4 cloves
2 tbsp clear honey
1 tbsp sliced almonds, toasted

NUTRITION NOTES	
Per portion:	
Energy	196Kcals/825kJ
Fat	2.84g
Saturated fat	0.41g
Cholesterol	0
Fiber	6.82g

1 Wash the kumquats and, if they are large, cut them in half. Place them in a saucepan with the apricots, golden raisins and water. Bring to a boil.

2 Pare the rind thinly from the orange, peel and grate the ginger, crush the cardamom pods and add to the pan, with the cloves.

3 Reduce the heat, cover the pan and simmer gently for about 30 minutes or until the fruit is tender.

4 Squeeze the juice from the orange and add to the pan with honey to sweeten to taste, sprinkle with sliced almonds, and serve warm.

COOK'S TIP
Use ready-to-eat dried apricots, but reduce the liquid to 1¼ cups, and add 5 minutes before the end.

BAKED APPLES IN HONEY AND LEMON

A classic mix of flavors in a healthy, traditional family dessert. Serve warm, with skim milk custard.

INGREDIENTS

Serves 4
4 cooking apples
1 tbsp clear honey
grated rind and juice of 1 lemon
2 tbsp low fat margarine

NUTRITION NOTES

Per portion:

Energy	71Kcals/299kJ
Fat	1.69g
Saturated fat	0.37g
Cholesterol	0.23mg
Fiber	1.93g

COOK'S TIP
Apples are divided into dessert (or eating) and cooking apples. While cooking apples can only be used for culinary purposes because they have a sour taste, some dessert apples, especially if firm, can be used in cooking. Look for smooth skinned apples and avoid any with brown bruises.

1 Preheat the oven to 350°F. Remove the cores from the apples, leaving them whole.

2 With a cannelle or sharp knife, cut lines through the apple skin at intervals and place in an ovenproof dish.

3 Mix together the honey, lemon rind and juice, and low fat margarine.

4 Spoon the mixture into the apples and cover the dish with foil or a lid. Bake for about 40–45 minutes, or until the apples are tender. Serve with custard made from skim milk.

COOK'S TIP
This recipe can also be cooked in the microwave to save time. Place the apples in a microwave-safe dish and cover them with a lid or pierced plastic wrap. Microwave on FULL POWER (100%) for about 9–10 minutes.

FRUITY BREAD PUDDING

A delicious family favorite from grandmother's day, with a lighter, healthier touch.

INGREDIENTS

Serves 4
⅔ cup mixed dried fruit
⅔ cup apple juice
1¼ cups stale whole-wheat or white bread, diced
1 tsp cinnamon
1 large banana, sliced
⅔ cup skim milk
1 tbsp raw sugar
plain low fat yogurt, to serve

1 Preheat the oven to 400°F. Place the dried fruit in a small pan with the apple juice and bring to a boil.

2 Remove the pan from the heat and stir in the bread, spice, and banana. Spoon the mixture into a shallow 5 cup ovenproof dish and pour over the milk.

3 Sprinkle with raw sugar and bake for 25–30 minutes, until firm and golden brown. Serve hot or cold with plain yogurt.

COOK'S TIP
Different types of bread will absorb varying amounts of liquid, so you may need to adjust the amount of milk to allow for this.

NUTRITION NOTES

Per portion:	
Energy	190Kcals/800kJ
Fat	0.89g
Saturated fat	0.21g
Cholesterol	0.75mg
Fiber	1.8g

BAKED BLACKBERRY CHEESECAKE

This light cheesecake is best made with wild blackberries, but cultivated ones will do. You can also substitute them for other soft fruit such as raspberries or loganberries.

INGREDIENTS

Serves 5
¾ *cup cottage cheese*
⅔ *cup plain low fat yogurt*
1 tbsp whole-wheat flour
2 tbsp golden caster sugar
1 egg
1 egg white
finely grated rind and juice of ½ lemon
2 cups blackberries

NUTRITION NOTES

Per portion:
Energy	94Kcals/394kJ
Fat	1.67g
Saturated fat	1.03g
Cholesterol	5.75mg
Fiber	1.71g

1 Preheat the oven to 350°F. Lightly grease and line the base of a 7in cake pan.

2 Whizz the cottage cheese in a food processor or blender until smooth, or rub it through a strainer.

3 Add the yogurt, flour, sugar, egg and egg white, and mix. Add the lemon rind and juice, and blackberries, reserving a few for decoration.

4 Tip the mixture into the prepared pan and bake it for about 30–35 minutes, or until just set. Turn off the oven and leave for 30 minutes.

5 Run a knife around the edge of the cheesecake, and then turn it out.

6 Remove the lining paper and place the cheesecake on a warm serving plate. Decorate with the reserved blackberries and serve it warm.

COOK'S TIP
If you prefer to use canned blackberries, choose those preserved in natural juice and drain the fruit well before adding it to the cheesecake mixture. The juice may be served with the cheesecake, but this will increase the total calories.

HOT PLUM BATTER

Other fruits can be used in place of plums, depending on the season. Canned black cherries are also a convenient pantry substitute.

INGREDIENTS

Serves 4

1 lb ripe red plums, quartered and pitted
⅞ cup skim milk
4 tbsp skim milk powder
1 tbsp brown sugar
1 tsp vanilla extract
3oz self-rising flour
2 egg whites
confectioners' sugar, to sprinkle

1 Preheat the oven to 425°F. Lightly oil a wide, shallow ovenproof dish and add the plums.

2 Pour the milk, milk powder, sugar, vanilla, flour, and egg whites into a food processor. Process until smooth.

3 Pour the batter over the plums. Bake for 25–30 minutes, or until puffed and golden. Sprinkle with confectioners' sugar and serve hot.

NUTRITION NOTES

Per portion:

Energy	195Kcals/816kJ
Fat	0.48g
Saturated fat	0.12g
Cholesterol	2.8mg
Fiber	2.27g

GLAZED APRICOT PUDDING

British-style puddings are usually very high in saturated fat, but this one uses the minimum of oil and no eggs.

INGREDIENTS

Serves 4

2 tsp golden syrup
14oz can apricot halves in fruit juice
1¼ cup self-rising flour
1½ cups fresh bread crumbs
⅔ cup brown sugar
1 tsp ground cinnamon
2 tbsp sunflower oil
¾ cup skim milk

1 Preheat the oven to 350°F. Lightly oil a cup pudding bowl. Spoon in the syrup.

2 Drain the apricots and reserve the juice. Arrange about 8 halves in the basin. Purée the rest of the apricots with the juice and set aside.

3 Mix the flour, bread crumbs, sugar, and cinnamon, then beat in the oil and milk. Spoon into the bowl and bake for 50–55 minutes, or until firm and golden. Turn out and serve with the puréed fruit as a sauce.

NUTRITION NOTES

Per portion:

Energy	364Kcals/1530kJ
Fat	6.47g
Saturated fat	0.89g
Cholesterol	0.88mg
Fiber	2.37g

Pears in Maple and Yogurt Sauce

Ingredients

Serves 6

6 firm pears
15ml/1 tbsp lemon juice
250ml/8fl oz/1 cup sweet white wine or
   cider
thinly pared rind of 1 lemon
1 cinnamon stick
30ml/2 tbsp maple syrup
2.5ml/½ tsp arrowroot
150g/5oz/⅔ cup low fat Greek-style
   yogurt

Nutrition Notes

Per portion:

Energy	132Kcals/556kJ
Fat	2.4g
Saturated fat	1.43g
Cholesterol	3.25mg
Fibre	2.64g

1 Thinly peel the pears, leaving them whole and with stalks intact. Brush them with lemon juice, to prevent them from browning. Use a potato peeler or small knife to scoop out the core from the base of each pear.

2 Place the pears in a wide, heavy saucepan and pour over the wine or cider, with enough cold water almost to cover the pears.

3 Add the lemon rind and cinnamon stick, and then bring to the boil. Reduce the heat, and simmer the pears gently for about 30–40 minutes, or until tender. Turn the pears occasionally. Lift the pears out carefully, draining them well.

4 Bring the liquid to the boil and boil uncovered to reduce to about 120ml/4fl oz/½ cup.

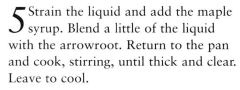

5 Strain the liquid and add the maple syrup. Blend a little of the liquid with the arrowroot. Return to the pan and cook, stirring, until thick and clear. Leave to cool.

6 Slice each pear about three-quarters of the way through, leaving the slices attached at the stem end. Fan each pear out on a serving plate.

7 Stir 30ml/2 tbsp of the cooled syrup into the yogurt and spoon it around the pears. Drizzle with the remaining syrup and serve immediately.

Cook's Tip

Poach the pears in advance, and have the cooled syrup ready to spoon on to the plates just before serving. The cooking time of this dish will vary, depending upon the type and ripeness of the pears. The pears should be ripe, but still firm – over-ripe ones will not keep their shape well.

RASPBERRY-PASSIONFRUIT SWIRLS

If passionfruit is not available, this simple dessert can be made with raspberries alone.

INGREDIENTS

Serves 4

2½ cups raspberries
2 passionfruit
1⅔ cups low fat fromage frais
2 tbsp sugar
raspberries and sprigs of mint, to decorate

1 Mash the raspberries in a small bowl with a fork until the juice runs. Scoop out the passionfruit pulp into a separate bowl with the fromage frais and sugar and mix well.

2 Spoon alternate spoonfuls of the raspberry pulp and the fromage frais mixture into stemmed glasses or one large serving dish, stirring lightly to create a swirled effect.

3 Decorate each dessert with a whole raspberry and a sprig of fresh mint. Serve chilled.

COOK'S TIP
Over-ripe, slightly soft fruit can also be used in this recipe. Use frozen raspberries when fresh are not available, but thaw first.

NUTRITION NOTES

Per portion:

Energy	110Kcals/462kJ
Fat	0.47g
Saturated fat	0.13g
Cholesterol	1mg
Fiber	2.12g

CHERRY CRÊPES

INGREDIENTS

Serves 4
½ cup flour
⅓ cup whole-wheat flour
pinch of salt
1 egg white
⅔ cup skim milk
⅔ cup water
1 tbsp sunflower oil, for frying
low fat ricotta cheese, to serve

For the filling
15oz can black cherries in juice
1½ tsp arrowroot

NUTRITION NOTES

Per portion:
Energy	173Kcals/725kJ
Fat	3.33g
Saturated fat	0.44g
Cholesterol	0.75mg
Fiber	2.36g

1 Sift the flours and salt into a bowl, adding any bran left in the sifter to the bowl at the end.

2 Make a well in the center of the flour and add the egg white. Gradually beat in the milk and water, whisking hard until all the liquid is incorporated and the batter is smooth and bubbly.

3 Heat a nonstick frying pan with a small amount of oil until the pan is very hot. Pour in just enough batter to cover the base of the pan, swirling the pan to cover the base evenly.

4 Cook until the crêpe is set and golden, and then turn to cook the other side. Remove to a sheet of paper towel and then cook the remaining batter, to make about eight pancakes.

5 For the filling, drain the cherries, reserving the juice. Blend about 2 tbsp of the juice from the can of cherries with the arrowroot in a saucepan. Stir in the rest of the juice. Heat gently, stirring, until boiling. Stir over a moderate heat for about 2 minutes, until thickened and clear.

6 Add the cherries to the sauce and stir until thoroughly heated. Spoon the cherries into the crêpes and fold them into quarters.

COOK'S TIP
If fresh cherries are in season, cook them gently in enough apple juice just to cover them, and then thicken the juice with arrowroot as in Step 5. The basic crêpes will freeze very successfully between layers of paper towel or waxed paper.

APRICOT AND ORANGE ROULADE

This elegant dessert is very good served with a spoonful or two of plain yogurt.

INGREDIENTS

Serves 6
4 egg whites
½ cup golden superfine sugar
½ cup flour
finely grated rind of 1 small orange
3 tbsp orange juice
2 tsp confectioner's sugar and shreds of orange zest, to decorate

For the filling
⅓ cup ready-to-eat dried apricots
⅓ cup orange juice

NUTRITION NOTES

Per portion:
Energy	203Kcals/853kJ
Fat	10.52g
Saturated fat	2.05g
Cholesterol	0
Fiber	2.53g

1 Preheat the oven to 400°F. Lightly grease a 9 x 13in jelly roll pan and line it with nonstick parchment paper. Grease the paper.

2 For the roulade, place the egg whites in a large bowl and whisk them until they hold soft peaks. Gradually add the sugar, whisking hard between each addition.

3 Fold in the flour, orange rind and juice. Spoon the mixture into the prepared pan and spread it evenly.

4 Bake for about 15–18 minutes, or until the sponge is firm and light golden in color. Turn out on to a sheet of nonstick parchment paper and roll it up jelly roll-style loosely from one short side. Leave to cool.

5 For the filling, roughly chop the apricots, and place them in a saucepan with the orange juice. Cover the pan and leave to simmer for a few minutes until most of the liquid has been absorbed. Purée the apricots in a food processor or blender.

6 Unroll the roulade and spread with the apricot mixture. Roll up, then arrange strips of paper diagonally across the roll, sprinkle lightly with confectioner's sugar, remove the paper and scatter with orange zest to serve.

COOK'S TIP
Make and bake the sponge mixture a day in advance and keep it, rolled with the paper, in a cool place. Fill it with the fruit purée 2–3 hours before serving. The sponge can also be frozen for up to 2 months; thaw it at room temperature and fill it as above.

SUNFLOWER-RAISIN SCONES

INGREDIENTS

Makes 10–12

2 cups self-rising flour
1 tsp baking powder
2 tbsp soft sunflower margarine
2 tbsp sugar
⅓ cup raisins
2 tbsp sunflower seeds
⅔ cup plain yogurt
about 2–3 tbsp skim milk

1 Preheat the oven to 450°F. Lightly oil a baking sheet. Sift the flour and baking powder into a bowl and rub in the margarine evenly.

2 Stir in the sugar, raisins, and half the sunflower seeds, then mix in the yogurt, with just enough milk to make a fairly soft, but not sticky dough.

3 Roll out on a lightly floured surface to about ¾ in thickness. Cut into 2½ in flower shapes or rounds with a cookie cutter and lift onto the baking sheet.

4 Brush with milk and sprinkle with the reserved sunflower seeds, then bake for 10–12 minutes, until puffed and golden brown.

5 Cool the scones on a wire rack. Serve split and spread with jam or low fat spread.

NUTRITION NOTES

Per portion:	
Energy	176Kcals/742kJ
Fat	5.32g
Saturated fat	0.81g
Cholesterol	0.84mg
Fiber	1.26g

PRUNE AND CANDIED PEEL BUNS

INGREDIENTS

Makes 12

2 cups flour
2 tsp baking powder
⅔ cup raw sugar
½ cup chopped dried prunes
⅓ cup chopped candied citrus peel
finely grated rind of 1 lemon
¼ cup sunflower oil
5 tbsp skim milk

NUTRITION NOTES

Per portion:	
Energy	135Kcals/570kJ
Fat	3.35g
Saturated fat	0.44g
Cholesterol	0.13mg
Fiber	0.86g

1 Preheat the oven to 400°F. Lightly oil a large baking sheet. Sift together the flour and baking powder, then stir in the sugar, prunes, peel, and lemon rind.

2 Mix the oil and milk, then stir into the mixture, to make a dough which just binds together.

3 Spoon coarse mounds onto the baking sheet and bake for 20 minutes, until golden. Cool on a wire rack.

SAFFRON FOCCACIA

A dazzling yellow bread with a distinctive flavor.

INGREDIENTS

Makes 1 loaf
pinch of saffron threads
⅔ cup boiling water
2 cups flour
½ tsp salt
1 tsp fast-rising dried yeast
1 tbsp olive oil

For the topping
2 garlic cloves, sliced
1 red onion, cut into thin wedges
rosemary sprigs
12 black olives, pitted and coarsely chopped
1 tbsp olive oil

NUTRITION NOTES

Per loaf:	
Energy	1047Kcals/4399kJ
Fat	29.15g
Saturated fat	4.06g
Cholesterol	0
Fiber	9.48g

1 Place the saffron in a heatproof cup and pour on the boiling water. Leave to stand and infuse the saffron until lukewarm.

2 Place the flour, salt, yeast and olive oil in a food processor or blender. Gradually add the saffron and its liquid until the dough forms a ball.

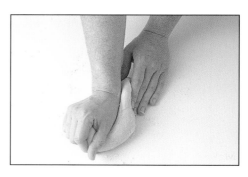

3 Turn out on to a floured board and knead for 10–15 minutes. Place in a bowl, cover and leave to rise for about 30–40 minutes until doubled in size.

4 Punch down the risen dough on a lightly floured surface and roll out into an oval shape, ½in thick. Place on a lightly greased cookie sheet and leave to rise for 20–30 minutes.

5 Preheat the oven to 400°F. Use your fingers to press small indentations over the surface.

6 Cover with the topping ingredients, brush lightly with olive oil, and bake for about 25 minutes or until the loaf sounds hollow when tapped on the bottom. Leave to cool.

TOMATO BREADSTICKS

Once you've tried this simple recipe you'll never buy manufactured breadsticks again. Serve as a snack, or with aperitifs and a dip at the beginning of a meal.

── INGREDIENTS ──

Makes 16

2 cups flour
½ tsp salt
½ tbsp fast-rising dried yeast
1 tsp clear honey
1 tsp olive oil
⅔ cup warm water
6 halves sun-dried tomatoes in olive oil, drained and chopped
1 tbsp skim milk
2 tsp poppy seeds

── NUTRITION NOTES ──

Per portion:	
Energy	82Kcals/346kJ
Fat	3.53g
Saturated fat	0.44g
Cholesterol	0
Fiber	0.44g

1 Place the flour, salt and yeast in a food processor or blender. Add the honey and olive oil and, with the machine running, gradually pour in the water (you may not need it all as flours vary). Stop adding water as soon as the dough starts to cling together. Process for 1 minute more.

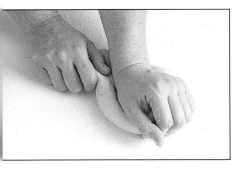

2 Turn out the dough on to a floured board and knead for 3–4 minutes until springy and smooth.

3 Knead in the chopped sun-dried tomatoes. Form into a ball and place in a lightly oiled bowl. Leave to rise for 5 minutes.

4 Preheat the oven to 300°F. Divide the dough into sixteen pieces and roll each piece into a 11 x ½in long stick. Place the sticks on a lightly oiled cookie sheet and leave to rise in a warm place for 15 minutes.

5 Brush the sticks with milk and sprinkle with poppy seeds. Bake for 30 minutes. Leave to cool on a wire cooling rack.

> **COOK'S TIP**
> Instead of sun-dried tomatoes, you could try making these breadsticks with reduced fat Cheddar cheese, sesame seeds or fresh chopped herbs.

INDEX